Generation Dubai
Exit, Voice and Loyalty

Khezri Collection

Generation Dubai
Exit, Voice and Loyalty
Bijan Khezri

To Ileen

As Rickie said in 'Casablanca':
"This is the beginning of a
beautiful friendship..."

Khezri Collection

British Library Cataloguing-in-Publication Data A British Library CIP record is available.

ISBN 978-0-9561164-0-6

Grateful acknowledgement is made to the following for permission to print:
Charles Avery
   Plane of the Gods, 2006 (Copyright Charles Avery; Courtesy Khezri Collection)
   Ridable, 2008 (Copyright Charles Avery)
Hendrik Krawen
   Adam und Eva, 2005 (Copyright Hendrik Krawen; Courtesy Khezri Collection)

Design: Joanna Deans, Identity, United Kingdom
Origination: DL Interactive, United Kingdom
Printing: die Keure, Brugge, Belgium

www.generationdubai.com

for Mila, Alexi and Stella

Table of Contents

Acknowledgement

I have made strong claims. Should those claims be proven wrong, I deserve severe criticism. I have built upon the work of others and have benefited from the invaluable criticism of my wife Mila and friends, in particular, Syed Albukhary, Johannes Bohnen, Hussein Chahine, Martin Jetter, Howard Jones, Larry Levy and Kay Pallister. I am deeply indebted to all of them for their constructive comments, and any shortcomings are entirely theirs.

If the book succeeds stimulating reflection and debate, I shall be grateful.

Charles Avery, *Plane of the Gods*, 2006

"Imagine time as a river, and that we are flying high above it in an aeroplane. Far below you can just make out the mountain caves of mammoth-hunters, and the steppes where the first cereals grew. Those distant dots are the pyramids and the Tower of Babel. In these lowlands the Jews once tended their flocks. This is the sea the Phoenicians sailed across. What looks like a white star shining over there, with the sea on either side, is in fact the Acropolis, the symbol of Greek art. And there, on the other side of the world, are the great, dark forests where the Indian penitents withdrew to mediate and the Buddha experienced Enlightenment. Now we can see the Great Wall of China and, over there, the smoldering ruins of Carthage. In those gigantic stone funnels the Romans watched Christians being torn to pieces by wild beasts. The dark clouds on the horizon are the storm clouds of the Migrations, and it was in those forests, beside the river, that the first monks converted and educated the Germanic tribes. Leaving the deserts over there behind them, the Arabs set out to conquer the world, and this is where Charlemagne ruled. On this hill the fortress still stands where the struggle between the pope and the emperor, over which of them was to dominate the world, was finally decided. We can see castles from the Age of Chivalry and, nearer still, cities with beautiful cathedrals – over there is Florence, and there the new St. Peter's, the cause of Luther's quarrel with the Church. The city of Mexico is on fire, the Invincible Armada is being wrecked off England's coast. That dense smoke comes from burning villages and the bonfires on which people were burnt during the Thirty Years War. The Magnificent chateau set in a great park is Louis XIV's Palace of Versailles. Here are the Turks encamped outside Vienna, and nearer still the simple castles of Frederick the Great and Maria Theresa. In the distance the cries of 'Liberty, Equality and Fraternity' reach us from the streets of Paris, and we can already see Moscow burning over there, and the wintry land in which the soldiers of the Last Conqueror's Grand Armee perished. Getting nearer, we can see smoke rising from factory chimneys and hear the whistle of railway trains. The Peking summer palace lies in ruins, and warships are leaving Japanese ports under the flag of the rising sun. Here, the guns of the World War are still thundering. Poison gas is drifting across the land. And over there, through the open dome of an observatory, a giant telescope directs the gaze of an astronomer towards unimaginably distant galaxies. But below us and in front of us there is nothing but mist, mist that is dense and impenetrable."

E.H. Gombrich, *A Little History of the World (1936)*

Prologue

"History is nothing but a procession of false Absolutes, a series of temples raised to pretexts, a degradation of the mind before the Improbable."

E.M. Cioran, *A Short History of Decay (1949)*

Early November 2008 -- The can-do spirit that for the past two decades so characteristically defined deregulation-driven growth in finance is under attack as the descending tide of an asset bubble is stranding a world of failed banks and over-indebted consumers. The Western world appears to have been fueled by a reckless pursuit of material enrichment in the absence of underlying substance as well as appropriate regulatory oversight. There are few places other than Dubai that have come to so perfectly embody this spirit of unstoppably pushing beyond conventional boundaries in time and space – indeed, often with little regard for its sustainability.

Whether Dubai, too, in the end, will fall victim to a self-inflicted asset bubble is irrelevant for the purposes of this book. But we must defend – against the West's dominating bureaucratic encroachment – the spirit that celebrates and encourages dreaming and eventually realizing the *Improbable*. It is this spirit that is the foundation of Dubai's historic development and magnetism. And it is a spirit that has been largely suffocated – and partly altogether lost – in Western democracies.

Exit, Voice and Loyalty, Nobel laureate Albert Hirschman's 1970 landmark publication, sponsors the conceptual framework to understand how the individual's responses to the decaying forces that inflict today's Western democratic model and society have given birth to new places such as Dubai. Dubai's rise, irrespective of its sustainability, is inseparable from the West's perishing appeal as a destination to fulfill one's professional and material ambitions. As more and more individuals *Exit* the West for brighter places, *Voice* – civic engagement – has lost its meaning in a democratic system that is struggling to serve its citizens. The growing feasibility of *Exit* undermines *Loyalty*.

The world has reached an inflection point. Determined to break with a repetition in futility, an emerging generation is longing for something new. US President-elect Barack Obama is a potent symbol of this desire, beyond America, to break with the past and envision a new and better world.[1]

Following the horrific events that mark September–11, 'What went wrong?' was the central question. There was hope that a better understanding will eventually set the world straight – in the end, little changed. Today, the credit crisis has caught most people in disbelief, too. But Western governments will struggle to address the short-term imbalances while laying a long-term foundation for future growth, unless prevalent governance and fiscal models are fundamentally reconsidered. Both events reveal the limitations of our understanding, imagination and choices.

Three questions define the transition from old to new. All three questions revolve around one essential theme: the dilemmas that oppose self and society in a world where survival – professionally, materially and spiritually – is more and more determined by personal choices that reach beyond conventional boundaries.

Does democracy deliver the public goods the electorate longs for? Democracy has failed on its promises, jubilantly reignited in 1989. Its latest faltering advancement across the globe is not a victory for its opponents but Western democracy's inherent tendency to turn against itself as it produces sub-optimal choices and outcomes. In advanced democracies, *Voice*, best embodied in the vote of a politically emancipated electorate, is less and less meaningful. The mature democratic system, in most countries, has been hijacked by the exigencies of political parties' power ambitions, lobbyists' rent-seeking or, for that matter, politicians' obsessive self-centrism around single causes that do not necessarily advance citizens' priorities. In particular, in Europe where an electorate is feeling more and more disenfranchised by the distant and all-powerful European Union's bureaucracy, the seeds of anti-systemic resentment have been sown. *Exit*, in search for places that put a combination of private wealth-creation, personal self-fulfillment and competitive public services first, has undermined the relevance of *Voice*. At no time in the history of democracy has the citizen been farther removed from self-government – democracy's very postulate – than today. And against this background we must not only question altogether the feasibility of 'self-government' but judge the increasing acceptability that authoritarian capitalism, at least for now, is enjoying in many parts of the world. The credit crisis and the related government responses that follow will further reinforce the decaying state of Western democracy's governance model.

How real is a clash of civilizations? Conflicts over political power interests rather than differences in religion, culture and ideology are the driving force behind terror, war and tension. Nonetheless, in a globalized world, an individual's identity is more and more defined in terms of cultural as well as religious belonging rather than nationality and *Voice*. Dubai is a powerful example of peaceful civilizational co-existence, in particular between Islam and Western values. Some commentators, however, believe that this peaceful co-existence is under threat.

But the threat emanates from a doctrinaire minority that is sidelined with no participation in the current arrangement of economic power sharing. It is a power struggle.

How important is location in a flattening world or "Who's Your City?"[2] What used to be the dividing line between the rural and the urban within one country has become a transnational fault line between the *rooted* and the *mobile* across the globe. Socio-economic progress is more and more dependent on the individual's ability to move to the *right* location. When the Chief Executive of a blue-chip US conglomerate moves part of his office to Dubai[3], it emphasizes the spikiness[4] of a flat world. But it also portrays a world where *Loyalty* to any particular location, system or organization is in decay. There are fewer and fewer rewards for *Loyalty* as agility determines survival and competitiveness. The socio-economic consequences are vast as economic structures and industrial clusters can shift overnight, leaving those behind that are not prepared to adopt change as a basic value. The *mobile* are no longer just a *Lonely Crowd* of "rootless cosmopolitans addicted to visions of wealth", but will define the norm and drive the dynamics of economic change.

This book is an essay, without scholarly presumptions. I want to take the reader on a flight and stimulate a personal journey of reflection confronting one's sense of history, belonging and direction. Historical consciousness is a powerful navigation tool for self-fulfillment. However difficult to capture in empirical evidence it may be today, in a world that appears to be fluid and globally intertwined, the individual is increasingly craving for purpose.[5]

A mix of futile decadence, soul-searching and a reawakened animal faith to create something new is setting the scene at what appears to be the dawn of a new age. Dubai is the ultimate embodiment of Western decadence. And decadence can seed the grounds for revolutions. Independently of whether the 'undreamed-of-new' will eventually be born on Dubai's soil, Dubai's historical mark on the modern world will be undeniable. The force of dreaming the *Improbable* that has so characteristically profiled Dubai's can-do spirit, must survive – beyond Dubai. It is inseparably linked not only to Dubai's existence, but the birth of the modern world.

Without the encouragement and guidance of my wife Mila, this book would have been impossible. And if it wasn't for my wife, I may have never considered the photos – spontaneously and randomly taken for her in Dubai in September 2007 – to capture the spirit of a world in transition. I have adopted the layout she had put together for a private book print – *Drive-By Dubai in 2007*. The photos document a massive construction site where the contours of the new are still misty.

Generation Dubai is dedicated to her and our children Alexi and Stella.

An Introduction

"And they said, Go to, let us build us a city and a tower, whose top may reach unto heaven; and let us make us a name, lest we be scattered abroad upon the face of the whole earth. And the Lord said, Behold, the people is one.... and this they begin to do: and now nothing will be restrained from them, which they have imagined to do..."

The Bible, Genesis 11:4,6 (King James Version)

The very decadence Dubai, one of the seven emirates and the biggest city of the United Arab Emirates (UAE), has come to represent allows us to depict the extreme forces of the Western spirit – positive and negative – as well as the longing for something new at what appears to define a world in transition.

For *Generation Dubai*, the concepts of time and space are uprooted. For those that look and move forward, nationhood has lost its potency to instill a sense of belonging. The local and indigenous cultures have given way to a future-oriented and a-historic expatriatism. The individual's quest for identity and self-fulfillment are fuelled by a collective desire to conquer boundaries in time and space. The world is there to be acted upon. Authoritarian capitalism is increasingly acceptable as long as it promotes stability, protects property rights and facilitates the pursuit of private wealth in an environment of competitive public services in health, transport and education. "The whole world wants, not freedom, but EMANCIPATION and enjoyment."[6]

Dubai has become a metropolitan caricature of the celebrity culture that dominates today's Western world. The city extensively uses celebrities for the branding of events and property developments. But, moreover, Dubai aspires to be a celebrity in its own right. The city's astronomical rise, best illustrated by megalomaniac and sea-filling construction projects, has generated a level of mystical fame – constantly nurtured by a multifaceted public-relations machine. As is typical for most celebrities, the city has become a victim of a self-inflicted plight to keep the momentum going and rising.

So far, Dubai successfully continues to excercise a form of magnetism upon the rest of the world – from the Bangladeshi construction worker to the American Chief Executive. Their desire to stay varies. But they all believe that they are witnessing and are effectively part of a new experiment. Dubai's very foundation is built and continues to be dependent on the rest of the world opting for *Exit* rather than *Voice* – at least temporarily. Discontented Persians that left for Dubai in the 19th century to pursue their trade in the face of an invasive state at home, continue to represent Dubai's leading trading families today.

It is places like Dubai that have given new meaning to the individual's global mobility. More and more individuals in the West are choosing to *Exit* their respective home-countries in search for a better future abroad, rather than voicing change at home. And since there is less and less *Loyalty* to any particular place, country and system, this phenomenon will increasingly shape the face of global economic competition. Western democracies are challenged. The world may be flat thanks to technological developments. But the importance of location, nonetheless, is on the rise. And an individual's socio-economic advancement is more and more dependent on the ability to join the Club of the *mobile* embracing change and diversity across cultures and borders. For now, Dubai is the archetypical Club of the *mobile*, but not without a price.

Situated at the crossroads of the Middle East, Africa and Asia with a population of roughly 1.4 million residents – of whom more than 90% are expatriates[7] – and absorbing approximately an additional 25,000 every month[8] until recently, Dubai has emerged as the economic meeting point of East, West and Africa. With less than 200 years, Dubai's recorded history is short. But it is a story of vision, belief, determination and confidence in the future that has turned a non-existent fishing village surrounded by a camel-populated desert into one of the world's most *fantastic* places for trading, investment and lifestyle. It is the quintessential story of rags-to-riches.

The City's supercharged momentum started in the early 1960s when roads hardly existed and "transport within the town was possible only on donkey or camel."[9] It was the time when the publication of Herbert Marcuse's "One-Dimensional Man"[10] ignited a generation of students for revolts in the West – targeting consumer society's material affluence and conformism as well as lack of individualism – in fact, a one-dimensional 'society without opposition'.

Today, Dubai is the pan-ultimate society without opposition, dedicated to one mission: satisfy the Ruler's unquenchable appetite for setting new benchmarks in economic development where *the only limitations are your own limitations*. The resulting economic development model has served as an important foundation to foster the ruling family's power base. But as the rift between conservatively-minded Emiratis and the Westernized face of Dubai is growing, undoubtedly, more and more voices are questioning the domestic sustainability of the Dubai model.

It is the rather late discovery of – limited – oil reserves that forced Dubai to think and execute the *Improbable*: build a world-class port infrastructure, despite its coastline's shallow waters, to emerge as the world's leading trading hub. It has been the nature of war and tension debilitating its region that has reinforced Dubai's status as an oasis of opportunity and prosperity. Indeed, Dubai has been the inspirational force behind the rise of modern Qatar and Abu Dhabi – the new forces of global capitalism recycling massive oil and gas windfalls into significant stakes in the West's most prestigious industrial, banking and real estate assets. Whatever the future of Dubai, the one thing we cannot ever take from it is the trend-setting inspirational force it has represented to a new generation of economic strategic development adopted by an increasing number of countries and cities – beyond the Gulf.

The foundation of Dubai's success is many-sided, but its autocracy-rooted corporate approach to running the country is paramount. The pace of the world is increasingly short-term, but a government's ability to define and execute long-term and infrastructure-centric growth strategies is no less urgent. The governance of western democracies, as it now stands, is destined for an impasse as the system of checks-and-balances has turned into a feeding ground for politics' inherent short-term power aspirations hijacked by political parties and lobbyists.

Citizens' satisfaction with the quality or access to basic public services such as healthcare, education and transport is close to non-existent in most Western democracies. A citizen's political interest and engagement have vanished as the vote, or *Voice*, democracy's very foundation, is less meaningful in a system that is best caricatured by a self-feeding bureaucracy. Election manifestos are in most cases a calculated maneuvering to capture the electoral center-ground. Indeed, neither

Dubai-style autocracy nor Singapore's one-party democracy is the correct answer. But Western democracies' governance model has to become more corporate and results-oriented to re-conquer the hearts of the world.

Dubai's incredible success story, to date, is partly a mirror image of the failings of the West. Had the West not lost its magnetism and were the world not shifting eastwards, there would be no Dubai with the panache it has come to symbolize. And the implosion in Western credit markets, exposing the fragilities upon which democracy's "home-ownership society" allowed its banking system to prosper, will further discredit the West's governance model. Today, the West lacks a unique proposal to 're-found', beyond more regulations, the capitalistic system.

Historically, Dubai's magnetism has been uniquely fueled by an ambition to defy time and space. One may justifiably argue that it is exactly this spirit that allowed Western financial institutions to create an excessive off-balance sheet economy in structured financial products – beyond any regulatory supervision – that is today the root of the world's financial and, now, economic crisis.

Indeed, in the absence of a government's quasi-authoritarian ability to intervene abruptly and sweepingly to restore the conditions for balanced economic growth before a crisis hijacks the economy, this 'free-wheeling' spirit is potentially explosive. But nonetheless, it is that spirit of risk taking – albeit discredited today – that is at the heart of innovation and job creation.

In their respective responses to the credit crisis, the US and the UK offered two starkly different performances of democracy's governance model. The US rescue package has been flawed in nature to begin with. But, more importantly, it is compromised by political interests. In fact, any future analysis of the US's handling of the credit crisis must emphasize politics as a critical vector. Probably no later than when Lehman Brothers was forced into bankruptcy – following a weekend of failed discussions – were politics rather than sound judgment the master of conduct.

There appears to be little doubt that the UK's rescue package is superior in both nature and execution to that of the US. Instead of nationalizing 'toxic'[11] mortgage-related products, as the US' plan emphasized, the UK focused on the recapitalization of banks' balance sheets. But what really matters is the above-politics, results-driven and pragmatic approach – led by a Prime Minister who benefited from his long-standing experience as Chancellor of the Exchequer – that was displayed by the UK. It is that agility and effectiveness that should inspire long-term reforms of the Western governance model. Instead, when financial market volatility eventually normalizes and the crisis mode disperses, Western electorates are likely to be hit with a wave of excessive – and mostly ill-conceived[12] – regulations.

Democracy's party system has a tendency to institutionalize human nature's devilish herd instinct – to the point where the prospect of a non-partisan warning shot to avert a crisis is doomed to failure. In the absence of a severe crisis there is hardly any productive action. The West should finally acknowledge that the democratic governance model as it is currently practiced and treasured in the Western world is broken. The rent-seeking and partisan political compromises that have become the system's trademark not only fail to approximate optimal choices and results, but have left the electorate altogether disenfranchised.

Dubai is a microcosm that by the nature of its economic development – centered on low taxation, total openness and long-term public-private infrastructure investment models – can contribute to future debates around the Western governance model. Of course, the question arises whether Dubai's authoritarian leadership is prepared to address the excesses and imbalances that are likely to challenge its macro-economic advancement. But to judge by the historic track record of Dubai's ruling Maktoum family to successfully reinvent its development strategies and tactics – together with the massive financial backing of Abu Dhabi, the oil-rich capital of the UAE – there is a real chance that Dubai will prevent the worst and continue as one of the world's leading magnetic poles. Today, Dubai's challenge is the timing of sound analysis and creative policies. There certainly is no politicking to cloud determination and execution.

But for enthusiastic tourists and skeptical critics alike, Dubai remains above all a unique cocktail of Disneyland and Las Vegas, combining record-setting thematic mass entertainment with luxury decadence. For its critics, Dubai's credibility as a sustainable and reinvigorating force of the Western governance model is compromised by the absence of a democracy-based civic engagement and the prominent role it has played historically in laundering global cash, often from illicit activities. The sometimes life-threatening abuses of labor rights across the city's vast construction sector appear to be less of an issue today as international pressure groups from outside and within the UAE have fostered change.

In its race against time to attract the brightest, build the tallest and provide the world's most appealing life experience, Dubai, at times, appears to be overwhelmed. The City's high level of indebtedness illustrates the reflexes of a municipality that is likely punching above its true economic weight. Borrowing from sovereign and private creditors has been an integral part of Dubai's modern economic development, starting in 1958 with a £500,000 loan from Kuwait to dredge the creek's shallow waters for larger cargo ships.

But in the past years, leverage has taken on new proportions.[13] The Ruler of Dubai, Sheikh Mohammed, directly or indirectly controls a web of private and quasi-government investment companies that are set up to compete against each other, domestically as well as internationally. This culture of competition, the foundation of Dubai's economic spirit, has encouraged debt financing often resulting in excessive leverage. As the line between the ruler's and the government's assets is increasingly blurred,[14] it becomes more and more difficult for the outside world to truly assess how much free cash there really is in Dubai. If in doubt, there probably is not that much.

Today, more and more critics come forward to question the financial sustainability of an economic model that remains largely dependent on a combination of the Maktoum family's power base and the magnetism Dubai continues to exercise upon the rest of the world. While it all started with a split from Abu Dhabi in the 19th century, the interests between the two emirates are increasingly interlinked today. Indeed, it is not unthinkable that Abu Dhabi will be Dubai's financial white knight to protect "the city where the future starts" from the lethal consequences of overreaching in its quest to surpass everyone else.

There are other areas that raise questions about the maturity as well as sustainability of Dubai's success. The murky world of Dubai's justice system continues to provide rich content for media headlines like 'Detained banker 'tortured' in Dubai'[15] as the Government addresses a culture of corporate corruptions – at times directly implicating those with close connections to the Ruling Family. Questions around the likelihood and impact of a possible terrorist attack are on the rise[16] as a free-wheeling expatriatism is possibly eroding the city's Islamic foundation and may offend conservatives within the Emirates and extremists in the surrounding region. Projections of a property crash in around 2010 – the year when most existing developments will be completed – are gaining in weight as property developers are increasingly suspected of schemes engineering the appearance of success in the absence of sustainable sales momentum. As this book goes to print, the story of a falling Dubai property market starts making headlines.

The question that will occupy Dubai's admirers and critics alike is whether the City will succeed in developing a soul to foster self-identity beyond trade and investment and nourish expatriates' growing thirst for culture and spiritual self-fulfillment[17]. And more importantly, will it exercise humility to avoid the fate of the Tower of Babel? These questions are not only of relevance to Dubai but address an emerging global generation that essentially inaugurates the dawn of a new age. Driven by the challenge of survival, this generation is in search of something new as it attempts to conquer the moving boundaries of time and space. Indeed, it is a generation, which Dubai has come to perfectly symbolize: *Generation Dubai*.

Part I: At the End of an Age

"The careful historian, before he ventures to predict the course of history, murmurs to himself 'Schedel'. It is not a magic word, but the name of a learned German who, in 1493 – note the date – compiled and published the Nürnberg Chronicle. It announced that the sixth of the seven ages of mankind was drawing to a close, and it included several blank pages for recording anything of interest that might still occur during the final days. As we know, what occurred was the opening of the New World and all innovations that followed from it – hardly a close. With this risk in mind, I mean to set down what appears to me possible, plausible, likely as our own era reaches an end."

Jacques Barzun, *From Dawn to Decadence (2000)*

Introduction

Defining an age and determining its duration are tasks prone to controversy. The world's pace has been dramatically accelerating during the course of the 20th century. But distance in time and space remain vital to judging and contextualizing contemporary times. Indeed, the "shape and coloring of the next era is beyond anyone's power to define; if it were guessable it would not be new. But on the character of the interval between us and the real tomorrow, speculation is possible."[18] We must dare to judge the forces at play today.

Many obituaries have been written about the Modern Age. "What prompts so many commentators to speak of the 'end of history', of post-modernity…or otherwise to articulate the intuition of a radical change…is the fact that the long effort to accelerate the speed of movement has presently reached its 'natural limit.'"[19] Has it? To critically challenge the notion of progress is to question modernity. But "for the first time in two hundred years, more and more people, in more and more fields of life, have begun to question the still present and now outdated idea of 'Progress'."[20]

When in 1989 the Berlin Wall fell, it was instantly hailed as progress for humankind. For many, it was the long-awaited 'universal'[21] victory of Western values and ideas – in particular freedom and democracy. For others, it was the dawn of a new paradigm of international relations where "the fault lines between civilizations will be the battle lines of the future"[22] – with no guarantee for the West's supremacy.

Almost two decades after the fall of the Iron Curtain, the world appears to be less secure. But it also appears to be more real – more truthful. The ambitions of power are unveiled and naked – across the world. The question of the triumph of the West has become irrelevant. This is not 'closing time in the gardens of the West', to paraphrase Cyril Connolly's memorable phrase of 1949. In fact, the doors to the garden are not only wide open but the garden is enriched by unprecedented diversity and ever-accelerating mutations and shifts to the extent that it is as much the garden of the West as of the East.

Progress is not simply a matter of development of democratic institutions, scientific-technological or economic advancement. More than at any time since the dawn of modernity some two hundred years ago, progress is largely about the individual. How successfully will an individual adapt to constant change in a global and misty space? And yet, the world is still not as globally integrated as it was in 1914, before the outbreak of the Great War.

The economist John Maynard Keynes remembered the time before August 1914 "with wonder, as an era without exchange controls or customs barriers. You could bring anything you liked into Britain or send anything out. You could take any amount of currency with you when you traveled, or send (or bring back) any amount of currency; your bank did not report it to the government, as it does today. And if you decided to invest any amount of money in almost any country abroad, there was nobody whose permission had to be asked, nor was permission needed to withdraw that investment and any profits it may have earned when you wanted to do so."[23]

The outbreak of war in 1914 led to the dissolution of the Ottoman Empire and created the modern Middle East. A traditionally tribal population was artificially divided along quasi-national and, hence, unsustainable boundaries. The 1919 Versailles Peace Treaty celebrated ethnocentric nationhood as the foundation of a sovereign state's self-identity and as a result – involuntarily – turned the 20th century into humanity's bloodiest. Barbarian atrocities in the name of ethnic identity – and often committed by democracies – became the 20th century trademark.

In 1989, after the West's triumph over dictatorship, some believed that history had come to an end. The world was now destined for a peaceful world revolution of the market democracy. But this moment of triumph was short-lived. In the summer of 1991, the disintegration of former Yugoslavia – itself an artificial construct resulting from the ultimate consequences of the Treaty of Versailles – was the earliest indication that the forces of history were not dead but had only been anesthetized by dictatorship's iron rule.

Ex-Yugoslavia's genocide stunned the world and, in particular, Europe. In our minds, the reality of Nazi Germany's gas chambers rendered impossible genocide on European soil, ever again. We were wrong. And we could be proven wrong again. "The history of the last century showed the ease with which historical transformations of unprecedented violence could follow without warning on the heels of the best times."[24] History, and for that matter democracy, are not necessarily evolving along a continuum of benign progress. Regressions are frequent.

Our closing age – dominated by the West and characterized by an obsession with democracy and nationalism – started sometime around the end of the Great War in 1918. In fact, it was an age that emerged from *Exit* as hordes of Europeans continued their departure for America in search of prosperity and freedom. But it was an age predominantly captured by *Voice*, or the *Revolt of the Masses*.[25]

Following its final boost in 1989, this age is now approaching its end.[26] The emphasis is back on the individual and one's personal rather than collective choices. *Voice* or Democracy will play a less prominent role in the mindset and self-identity of the new emerging age. While Obama's victory has, undoubtedly, revalued the power of *Voice* – at least for a moment, civic engagement will take life less in the form of voter-participation, but is more and more of a charitable or environment-centric nature, dedicated to particular causes across national and religious boundaries. More importantly, the new age is no longer dominated by the West and Western values.

The new age is about pragmatism and will be primarily concerned with personal self-fulfillment, private wealth creation and spirituality – indifferent to location, the brand of the governance system or any particular religion. The fault line is neither between countries nor East-West or North-South, but runs straight through each society – pitting those fearful of change as well as deprived of means and self-confidence against those that embrace the opportunities the world has to offer, and if need be by moving abroad, *Exit*.

Little, if any, *Loyalty* is likely to be left for an ending age that, in its closing chapter, starts questioning the blind faith in democracy and dismantles misleading concepts such as *Clash of Civilizations* and *A Flat World*. The West is challenged to redefine its self-identity.

Democracy Turning Against Itself: From Kohl to Sarkozy

In 1983, the government of the Federal Republic of Germany, then led by newly elected Chancellor Helmut Kohl, supported the US's determination to station cruise missiles on German soil – amid strong resistance not only among large parts of Germany's population but within Kohl's party ranks, too. At the time, few believed that the Soviet Union would stage a military attack against the West. And therefore few were inclined to continue a costly arms race.

But Kohl's stance was a symbolic statement in defense of freedom, the capitalistic world and his firm belief that pressure on the Soviet Block must continue for Germany to be eventually re-united. At the time, the firmness of his position in defense of the free capitalistic world deeply impressed me and somehow shaped my view of the world and my love for America – supposedly, the ultimate embodiment of freedom and capitalistic prosperity. In fact, the fall of the Berlin Wall in November 1989 was not only Kohl's moment of triumph but all hopes were placed on the US to set the world free.

In the spring of 1989, the air was filled with a scent of revolution. Students' aspirations for freedom and democracy were crushed at Beijing's Tiananmen Square in June. And throughout the summer, people from the oppressed Eastern and Central European communist states were increasingly storming the embassies of Western countries to seek asylum. Soon, massive street protests followed, in particular in East Germany, the former German Democratic Republic. Whereas in China the students' objective was political reform through *Voice*, the citizens of the former communist states considered their very system beyond repair. They just wanted to *Exit* in the absence of any *Loyalty* for a rotten system and regime. For them, first and foremost, freedom of movement, in particular to the West, was the central theme and desire.

When on November 9th the Wall fell, the besieged government of the former German Democratic Republic *broke* the news on TV. At the time, though, the broadcast was not without ambiguity. In fact, there was uncertainty and bewilderment as to whether the East German leadership was really prepared to *open the gates*. The people did not believe it until they successfully tested – that same night – their new freedom at hereto heavily militarized checkpoints dividing Berlin.

As we now know, the East's decision to open the border was not an act of capitulation but symptomatic of the late leadership's uncompromised determination to alleviate pressure following months of public street protests throughout Eastern and Central Europe, and to partly regain control of the course of history in their fight for survival.

Chancellor Helmut Kohl brilliantly seized the historic opportunity. He did so boldly and impatiently. Within weeks he published his *personal* 10-Point Plan mapping out the path to German unification. According to Kohl, re-unification had to be completed swiftly and absolutely. If not, a historic opportunity would be missed and Western security could be at stake. The world was caught on a tightrope juggling between chaos and the long-awaited world revolution of democracy. "[Kohl] recognized the opportunity in last year's East German revolution and grabbed it. He bamboozled all four of the occupying powers – including that arch-bamboozler Mikhail Gorbatchev – into accepting fast-forward unity more or less on his terms"[27] wrote The Economist in March 1990.

It is exactly that approach, personified by Helmut Kohl, that was about to shape the post-1989 political mindset – first in Europe and, no later than September 11, 2001, taking root in the US, too. It can be best characterized by the renaissance of the Leviathan state. Political leaders were about to assume a towering role, obsessed with the belief that a new vacuum had opened where the individual politician – democratically elected – can make history again. The politics of fear served as an effective governance tool. The individual politician's self-centered fears and aspirations rather than economic growth and job creation have been shaping the political agenda's priorities ever since. And the rapid growth of the financial services sector, on the back of a massive expansion of secondary trading in derivatives and swaps - with a turnover often reaching a multiple of a country's actual gross national product - provided a rich and welcome source of tax revenues.

In July 1990, less than one year after the fall of the Wall, the currency systems of East and West Germany were swiftly and uncompromisingly united at parity, one-to-one. Politically motivated guarantees of wage parity – to enliven the East and to protect the West from West-bound labor migration – accentuated the two systems' massive economic disparity. For Germany the consequences were disastrous and are noticeable to the present day as the country remains economically divided.

Germany had just started recovering from nearly two decades of sluggish growth, when the foundations of sustainable economic growth are challenged by the impact of the current credit crisis. The impact will be accentuated by the Federal Republic's governance system and its conduciveness to political paralysis. Agility is compromised by a two-tier legislative system, usually controlled by opposing political parties.

Today, almost two decades after the protests and freedom revolutions of 1989, it is unclear whether it is the citizens of Eastern Germany or the students of Beijing that are better off. The West's blind faith in democracy and freedom could well be the source of its unmaking.

In 1989, when blood was spilling Tiananmen Square and Mikhail Gorbatchev, then presiding over the still existent Soviet Union, was hailed on Western streets as freedom's champion, it would have been beyond the most cynical of our imaginations that less than three years thereafter, in March 1992, the editorial of the Financial Times writes: "Who was right: Mikhail Gorbatchev or Deng Xiaoping? On the face of it, recent events in what used to be the two great bastions of doctrinaire Marxism-Leninism appear to throw that question into stark relief. In the former Soviet Union, the collapse of communism has been accompanied by economic misery and social chaos. In parts of still-communist totalitarian China, however, a form of capitalism is thriving, bringing with it an economic boom and strongly improving living standards…, the lesson Deng drew from the overheating of the economy which preceded Tiananmen is that economic reform necessitates the maintenance of tight political control."[28]

Gorbatchev "failed to give the clear political leadership, the sense of direction, for which the rudderless Soviet people were begging" wrote the Financial Times in late August 1991, the day after the failed coup against Gorbatchev[29]. In December 1991, following Gorbatchev's dignified surrender of power and the official end of the Soviet Union, Viktor Erofeyev, a literary critic and writer declared: "[Gorbatchev] had just enough intelligence to change everything, but not enough to see that everything would be destroyed. He was bold enough to challenge his party, and cautious enough to let the party live until it lost its power. He had enough faith in communism to be named its head, but he [had] enough doubts about it to destroy it. If he had seen everything clearly, he would have not changed Russia."[30]

Following the fall of the Soviet Union in 1991, Russia was a high-profile victim of a mania for uncontrolled liberalization and democracy. Shock therapy, orchestrated by a group of eminent Harvard economists, in particular Jeffrey Sachs, who now prominently champions the fight against Third World poverty, had disastrous consequences for Russia. Impatiently and ignorant of Russia's specific circumstances as well as the dangers of liberalizing financial markets too quickly in the absence of a liberalized real economy, advisors and advisees were obsessed with the pursuit of making history. To secure multi-billion dollar transfers from the West, the case was powerfully made that Russia's democratic future and Western security were one and the same.[31]

In the midst of shock therapy, the US launched a US$4bn fund to aid Russian privatization. In April 1993, the US Treasury Secretary announced that "the scheme would free Russia's central bank of some of the burden of converting the huge oil, gas and other leading industries to private control."[32] Chrysta Freeland's "Sale of the Century"[33] is an extraordinary account of how shock therapy's privatization program, sponsored by the West, created the oligarchs, effectively concentrating unprecedented wealth and control of the countries' entire natural resources in the hands of a few, plunging the country into economic chaos and preparing Russia for authoritarian rule.

Today, there is reason to be concerned about the Russian Government's arbitrary respect for civil rights and the politicization of energy exports. Putin's presidency, however, has spearheaded stability, broadened wealth creation and largely institutionalized the respect for a private life. What yardstick shall be applied to measure progress? One certainly finds more happy people in the streets of Russia in 2008 than ten years ago – then, presumably, the apex of Russia's first democracy and free media. Undoubtedly, rich windfalls from high commodity prices have been critical

to Putin's reign. Falling commodity prices are likely to reveal – possibly in the near future – what has been truly and sustainably achieved.

In Continental Europe, designs for monetary and political integration dominated the national agenda ever since the 1992 Treaty of Maastricht outlined the terms and conditions for the creation of a monetary union and a new currency, the Euro. The timing and contents of the Maastricht Treaty were also influenced by politicians' – not citizens' – fear of a rising and possibly dominating reunified Germany that might alter Europe's balance of power. In July 1990, after striking an agreement with Gorbatchev to clear the path for German unification, "Kohl was asked if the Zheleznovodsk agreement[34] was a new Rapallo – a reference to the 1922 treaty between communist USSR and the Weimar Republic that paved the way for German rearmament after World War I."[35]

In particular Margaret Thatcher, at the time Britain's towering Prime Minister championing the virtues of a smaller state and a deregulated market – indeed, then the progressive antithesis of its time in Europe – was trapped in anti-German feelings as confirmed by the "seminar she held with several well-known experts on Germany. They had to explain to the Prime Minister that the countries of Eastern Europe actually wanted German investment and that this 'did not necessarily equate to subjugation'. [Her private secretary's memo of the seminar] alleged that abiding characteristics of the Germans, 'in alphabetical order', included 'aggressiveness, assertiveness, bullying, egotism, inferiority complex, sentimentality.'"[36]

As German unification was about to challenge the balance of power amongst Europe's leading economies, the European integration process was less concerned with economic growth and job creation than with the distribution and management of political powers amongst its leading members. Since the fall of the Berlin Wall, European political integration has obsessed Europe's entire political elite, in spite of reservations amongst the electorate. In fact, any political ambitions to advance European integration beyond the Common Market have unchained anti-systemic resentment amongst the electorate.

Almost a decade following the 1992 Maastricht Treaty, European policymakers – with one exception, the British – disregarded the evident lessons from German Monetary Union and successfully pressed forward with European Monetary Union (EMU) and the creation of the Euro, despite deep-seated economic divergences across its member states. Again, a political class, indifferent to economic costs, was obsessed with both making history as well as fossilizing the balance of economic power within the European Union (EU).

EMU is the most prolific product of a political elite blinded by a principled obsession, here European integration, and the pursuit of power-centric politicking. It is also an example of a bureaucratic apparatus taking a life of its own beyond the control of voters. So far, the benefits of EMU remain questionable, at best. The Euro continues to rob its members of a badly needed country-specific monetary adjustment tool.

There is hardly any European that will not grumble about how the Euro has materially increased living expenses in the absence of a rise in real wages matching the difference. For some reason, substantial price increases following the introduction of the Euro are nowhere to be found in inflation data. And for those at the low-end of the income scale as well as the elderly dependent on inflation-indexed pensions, the Euro has mandated a substantial change in spending habits and lifestyle. A combination of rising costs and stagnant wages is eroding purchasing power.

The people had no say in the establishment of EMU. But when in 2005 French and Dutch voters were offered a referendum to vote on the European Constitution – an initiative to politically integrate the member-states of the European Union in a form not too dissimilar from that of the United States of America – it was overwhelmingly rejected. Europe's leaders were caught in disbelief. For the first time, the train of unquestioned European integration was brought to a halt. The referendums allowed a certain revival of *Voice*, evocative of a mini revolt.

At the time, I wrote in a Wall Street Journal editorial that "since the fall of the Berlin Wall, Europe's relative weight in the world has been steadfastly declining in economic terms. Europe's governing elite has dedicated all of its political capital to the integration process as an end in its own right. Overdue structural reforms of national economies have been defied. Instead, grand political designs such as EMU, enlargement and lately the constitution, have been sold to the electorate as a golden egg that shelters its peoples from economic sacrifices while establishing a counterweight to the U.S. The EU, independently of whether one considers it too neo-liberal or too socialist, has become the epitome of Europe's decline."[37]

The question of whether there is a need for a Constitution or not to accommodate an ever-increasing European Union from 12 member-states at the time of German unification to 27 in 2008, and possibly increasing, is irrelevant. It is important to understand that the need for a more efficient organizational structure of the EU is the direct consequence of an over-reliance on bureaucracy in the first place. The EU is trapped in a self-feeding vicious circle.

European leaders' subsequent repackaging of the Constitution as the Lisbon Treaty is a continuous manifestation of a political class fighting for its survival as they try to focus on their core competency: institution-building. But this time they fall short of projects that can ignite the electorate's passion. Indeed, whenever the electorate gets a chance to directly vote on a specific EU-related subject, the message is clear: stop a self-aggrandizing bureaucracy and refocus political accountability on job creation.

Despite Ireland not even representing one percent of the EU's popular vote, its rejection of the Lisbon Treaty in a referendum in June 2008 is representative of Europe's larger population. But Europe's political elite is caught in disbelief again. The German interior minister moaned over "letting a few million Irish make decisions for 495m Europeans"[38]. The fact that the 495m were not given a vote is ignored. "In short, EU leaders will happily accept referendum results that tell them what they want to hear. But if the votes are unwelcome, they dismiss them as democratically meaningless," writes The Economist.[39] It is a crisis of both democracy and leadership.

Kohl defined a generation of political leadership in Europe that has been obsessed with institution-building as an end in its own right. German unification and European political integration – fostering peace and stability – will robotically stimulate economic prosperity – this has been the dominant belief. "This started after the second world war as a noble effort to end all possibility of war between Germany and France. It was twinned with the creation of a large area of liberal trade, in a world still full of restrictions."[40] Indeed, Europe, more than any other region in the world, has been war-torn for centuries and our generation should not take peace for granted.

But as "the original goals have been lost in the mists of time, the aim of 'more Europe' has been pursued by the leading group of politicians and bureaucrats for its own sake, even to extending to the Brussels level decisions that are left to the state level in the US".[41] The problem with the post-1989 political leadership – on both sides of the Atlantic – has been its failure to appreciate that the world is changing, independently of Europe or the United States.

One man – Nicolas Sarkozy – embodied hope that Europe's leadership can reinvent itself from within. When he was elected President of France in May 2007, he was dubbed 'France's chance' and the 'entrepreneurial president' who called for the 'rehabilitation of money' empowering the 'taste of the young for success'. When elected as president, Sarkozy represented the end of a Cold-War fashioned gerontocracy to a new political generation, offering the possibility of France to exert influence through modern magnetism rather than arrogance[42] – indeed, similar to what our expectations are of Barack Obama in the US today.

Whilst misleading in many regards, France is a suitable caricature for Europe. In its extremes, France is a tale of two, ostensibly, disconnected worlds. Its corporate sector is competitive, expansive and global. Large parts of its political class and electorate, though, together provide a prolific caricature of a categorical anti-Anglo-Saxon mental entrapment. France's policies are state-capitalistic and an unacceptably large part of its youth is unemployed and left behind the pace of the modern world. France is fearful to embrace any future beyond its direct control.

Following the French rejection of the EU Constitution in a referendum in 2005, the then newly-appointed prime minister Dominique de Villepin declared in his acceptance speech that "the French know it and tell it to us with force: globalization is not an ideal, it cannot be our destiny". Such myopic electoral empathy has become too characteristic of democracies, on both sides of the Atlantic. It not only severely cannibalizes a meaningful public discourse but fosters distrust and fear, leading the citizen to capitulate by either decaying in solitude or revolt, or leaving for a brighter future elsewhere. France has no shortage of either mindless street protests or brain-drain.

For France to set itself mentally free it must change its school books first. Stefan Theil, Newsweek's European economics editor, undertook a valuable study of school textbooks in France and Germany.[43] A representative quote in one of the dominant textbooks, published in France in 2005 reads as follows: "Economic growth imposes a hectic form of life, producing overwork, stress, nervous depression, cardiovascular disease, and, according to some, even the development of cancer."[44]

It is hard to believe that democracies can produce such nonsense in the name of the state. With few exceptions, Continental Europe still profoundly despises capitalism but accepts it as part of freedom's package. The crisis afflicting financial markets in 2008 is lending credit to those voices resenting any capitalistic model that is beyond the direct tutelage of the state. The wave of regulatory activism certain to dominate the years to come will further expose Europe's inner conflict with capitalism. And Sarkozy is unlikely to miss the opportunity to champion 're-founding the capitalist system'[45] as he secures a global platform for himself, beyond France and possibly his own presidency.

Sarkozy's path to the presidency was branded by his aspiration to personify change, reinforced by his background as an outsider – "who owes nothing to anyone", in his own words. In fact, the up-coming political generation –

on both sides of the Atlantic – will be all about that *need for change* that the previous leadership had failed to both recognize and translate into policies. And a politician's individualism will be a potent election platform to lend credibility to break with past policies. While Kohl's obsession with institution-building was focused and based on principles and beliefs, Sarkozy embraces whatever is at hand and opportune to advance the 'independent' brand Sarkozy.[46] It is the ultimate parody of democracy's postulate of self-government.

Where Sarkozy emerges as a revealing caricature for democracy's current decay is in the force with which he has successfully exploited the electorate's ravenous appetite to enter the intimate sphere of anyone, but public figures in particular. The public sharing of his fast-paced private life in the name of political transparency cultivated a kind of individualism in public office that allowed him to become a celebrity in his own right, detached from the French presidency.[47] In a world where the boundaries between the public, private and intimate are increasingly blurred, Sarkozy exposes democracy's modern vulnerabilities.

Sarkozy "is the incarnation of the post-modern man, obsessed with himself, turned towards pleasure, autonomous and narcissistic. And he exhibits his joys and sorrows, all his private life, his sentimental doubts and pleasures. He represents the individualism of the society to the extreme – that's the individual who counts, not the society."[48] The presidency of Nicolas Sarkozy is likely to sketch the dangers of the twin-combination of a celebrity-culture infected individualism in politics paired with democracy's inability to effectively direct power towards change.

Democracy is the least evil of government systems, and possibly the best in terms of its ability to sustain continuity and peaceful succession in leadership. But democracy must reinvent itself and become more results-oriented, pragmatic and corporate in its governance approach. Election manifestos must become business plans – defined by principles and measured by performance benchmarks against spending. Once approved by the legislative, the executive must be fully empowered to execute with authority. Government spending must be capped as a percentage of gross national product for the governing period. Extraordinary spending beyond the initial 'business plan' requires legislative approval of a revised business plan authored by the executive.

During the governing period the legislative's primary responsibility is solely to ascertain the proper execution of the 'business plan' and that ad-hoc policy making is in accordance with established principles and objectives. This would reinstate the executive's accountability that is currently lost in today's mish-mash of pork-belly trading amongst lawmakers. Altogether, policy execution has to be re-centered around spending and results.

We also have to redefine the nature and role of the individual lawmaker. Similar to Switzerland's direct democracy, lawmakers should not be career politicians but must practice a profession outside of parliament. It is likely to take the 'glamour' out of lawmaking and will re-emphasize efficiency and results. Politicians' obsession with career within a political party is largely to be held responsible for modern democracy's decay. The lawmakers' quality of independence and analysis underlying political judgment is likely to be clouded by the party politics that have been allowed to solely define one's political existence and consciousness.

Do we need political parties? As the system now stands, it would not continue surviving without them. Political parties are the foundation of modern democracy. At a minimum, however, every parliament should include a certain number of lawmakers that have no historic or present affiliation with any one political party. Such mandate has the potential to reignite the electorate's interest and engagement in the political process. Modern media, blogging and social networking platforms have substantially reduced the individual's barriers and costs to entering politics if it wasn't for the gate-keeping of political parties.

Democracy's limitations and vulnerabilities have created a formidable environment for authoritarian capitalism to take centre-stage in today's world economy. A growing part of Western electorates start questioning whether democracy – as it now stands – is suitably equipped to deliver the public goods in healthcare, transport and education to protect and improve living standards. And democracies are no less vulnerable than autocracies to being hijacked by leaders' individualistic self-centrism around a particular agenda. Sarkozy aside, in 2003, Britain's former Prime Minister Tony Blair, single-handedly, led his country into war in Iraq – against the strong and unmistakable will of the British electorate at the time.

For now, history is unlikely to document 1989 as the beginning of an irreversible democratic world revolution, but more likely as Western democracies' peak. Democracy failed to deliver economic growth and job creation in Europe. And growth in the United States has quite dramatically polarized wealth-creation.

The consequences of the 2007 implosion in credit markets will serve as a catalyst to break the thin ice on which democracies and its leaders have operated for decades. With hardly any understanding of the implied systemic risks when allowing the financial services industry to prosper off-balance sheet in leverage-enhancing derivative products – despite the many warning signs during, at least, the past ten years – political leaders, more so than bankers, should be held to account. Simply more regulation – democracies' typical mantra – cannot be the right answer, though.

The Sarbanes-Oxley legislation in the US, for example, emotionally and hastily enacted to enhance corporate transparency after the collapse of US energy company Enron, has demonstrated the limitations as well as high cost[49] of any corporate and financial regulation that goes beyond the self-regulatory enforcement of sound principles. The credit crisis will rightly assault democracies' existing form and shape of capital markets governance. But any solution resulting from Western democracies' existing political processes is likely to be inadequate in the short-term and counterproductive in the long-run.

Financial regulation should follow the governance model of monetary policy. Most democracies have successfully de-politicized monetary policy by constitutionally protecting the independence of central banks in their mandate to pursue constitutionally set objectives. While some politicians, such as Sarkozy, would like to dilute that independence, the short history of central bank independence suggests that the electorate is best served when economic stewardship is not only insulated from politicians and politics, but governed by objectives and principles that are benchmarked against quantifiable measures.

Financial market regulation should be equally protected by a 'non-political', independent and unified authority that is driven by a principles-based regulatory approach. So far, the United Kingdom's Financial Services Authority is as good as it gets. But it still lacks sufficient independent powers.

Western democracies are in need of a fundamental constitutional reform that redefines not only the priorities of a modern economy but the mechanism that will allow approximating the objectives in the most straightforward way. However, it is unlikely to happen unless parliamentarians are prepared to question the very nature of their role and to envision a world where lawmaking is not monopolized by political parties. The global credit crisis presents a long-awaited opportunity to fundamentally question our governance system. We must reprogram a democracy model that appears to have lost its way.

Unless reformed, democracy – as a sought-after governance model – is unlikely to survive in its current practice, and authoritarianism is to further rise in prominence. The seeds for anti-systemic resentments have been sown in the West. *Exit* rather than *Voice* is an increasingly preferred option in an interconnected world where *Loyalty* to any particular place, system and ideology has lost its foundation. Today, places like Dubai are taking advantage of this discontent. Tomorrow, other places will be added. The West must re-conquer the space it started vacating no later than 1989.

No End to History: Clash *about* Civilization and the Struggle for Power

After more than four decades of Cold War, the fall of the Berlin Wall created a vacuum in many regards. Everyone was unprepared. The vacuum profiled most prominently is that the world was left with the United States as sole superpower – without any country or alliance to effectively counterbalance America's quest for military, economic and moral supremacy. The real vacuum, however, was in our minds. How to envision a world deprived of two rivaling power blocs, embodying, albeit with different success, two opposing visions of the nature of man, economic production and the course of history?

Two books have come to best symbolize the debate of the immediate post-Cold War era. For Francis Fukuyama history had come to an end as Western values and ideas attained undisputed universality.[50] For Samuel Huntington "The Clash of Civilizations"[51] was about to define the future. In fact, since the fall of the Berlin Wall's bipolar world, *Clash of Civilizations* turned out to be the most popular paradigm for analyzing conflicts across the world. And September-11, which like most of the major happenings of the twentieth century took the West by surprise, has been widely deemed to validate Huntington's outlook.

In the collective mind, 9-11 was accepted and is still perceived as the event that changed the world. Omnipresent security checks and discriminatory visa restrictions around the world have certainly altered everyone's travel experience. National security considerations have been upheld to ring-fence strategic assets from Arab control. In 2006, for example, the sale of the operations of six US ports to a state-owned company in Dubai, the US's most reliable and predictable ally in the Middle East, was blocked. But fundamentally, nothing much changed on September-11[52], other than our longing to better understand what has been going wrong, for apparently quite some time.

The day the World Trade Center – allegedly symbolic of the Tower of Babel – collapsed, the world was caught in shock. For the American people it was not only shock but disbelief. And the "disbelief underlies the a-historicity so characteristic of the American people."[53] No matter how persistent a theme political violence has been in American history, it "is not part of the consciousness and self-image of Americans."[54] The post 9-11 debate was dominated by explanations centered on simplistic dualisms such as good vs. evil, West vs. Islam, progress vs. regression – best summarized in a clash of civilizations. At the heart, though, is a bare power struggle for control of the Middle East, opposing the United States against, in particular, an Iran-led alliance.

Susan Sontag's comments, shortly after 9-11 widely regarded as callous and unpatriotic, appear to be more tolerable today, when she noted that the "disconnect between last Tuesday's monstrous dose of reality and the self-righteous drivel and outright deceptions being peddled by public figures and TV commentators is startling, depressing. The voices licensed to follow the event seemed to have joined together in a campaign to infantilize the public. Where is the acknowledgement that this was not a 'cowardly' attack on 'civilization' or 'liberty' or 'humanity' or 'the free world', but an attack on the world's self-proclaimed superpower, undertaken as a consequence of specific American alliances and actions?"[55] To understand is not to excuse.

Today, in fact, Muslims as well as non-Muslims believe that tensions between Islam and the West arise from conflicts over political power interests and not from differences in religion and culture, as a comprehensive survey by the BBC has documented.[56] Intolerant minorities, in all camps, rather than civilizations are to be blamed for conflict. "Indeed, the fiercest battle will be fought inside the Muslim world. That is where the revolution is taking place, and where it will have to be halted, preferably not by outside intervention, but by Muslims themselves."[57] Does Dubai offer a success model for the rest of the Arab world to aspire to?[58] It certainly is a valid question, entailing hope for a troubled region, but it ignores the very particular circumstances that drive Dubai's success.

At the dawn of the twentieth century "Americans, Englishmen and other westerners celebrated the growing triumph of civilized values. Shortly thereafter the world plunged into barbarism such as had never been seen before. Regressions are frequent."[59] And the enlightened West should always remember that Western democracies – rather than Islamic autocracies – turned the 20th century into humanity's bloodiest episode.

There is no guarantee that the individual, failing to navigate in the global space, will not regress into infancy and terror, again. In fact, modern terrorism is a form of such failure, where the individual finds refuge in radicalism and violence. If the "attraction of fascism, communism, and nationalism in the modern world has been their ability to provide a purpose in group solidarity for lives lacking an individual sense of meaning"[60] then Al Qaeda is modern globalization's fascism. It is a social and political, not a religious or cultural phenomenon.

Inspired by the scientific-industrial-technological revolution, a concept coined by anthropologist Ernest Gellner, the world is moving towards one civilization. But to call it the triumph of the West is not only preposterous but misguided. The world's economic epicenter has not only shifted eastwards but since the end of the 20th century this revolution has been more and more shaped by the East, in particular in regard to the world's growing appetite for spiritual nourishment. And the desert town Dubai – peacefully interweaving Islam and Western values – has, for now, become a caricature of a world converging towards *one* civilization. No other place but the United States has achieved this in modern history, so far.[61]

"This is not a clash between civilizations"[62], as former British Premier Blair noted in a speech in 2006. "It is a clash about civilization. It is the age-old battle between progress and reaction, between those who embrace and see opportunity in the modern world and those who reject its existence."[63] In fact, the division runs straight through Western society. It is this fault-line that will define one of the 21st century most demanding political priorities. History has not ended.[64]

The World is Flat: Pitting the *Mobile* against the *Rooted*

While the world is flattening, it is increasingly spiky[65], too. More and more hubs of economic, creative and cultural activity stand out. No question, 'flattening' technologies empower "individuals, in previously unheard-of ways, to reach farther, faster, deeper, and cheaper than ever before."[66] But – as paradoxical as it may appear – it is this phenomenon that is reinforcing the importance of location. In fact, global competitiveness is determined by the ability to de-root and re-cluster around a handful of key global centers. The phenomenon is not limited to individuals and businesses but cultural assets are not immune to the forces of location-centric globalization either.

In March 2007, Abu Dhabi, the political capital of the United Arab Emirates (UAE), agreed a joint-venture with France's Louvre and paid more than $1 billion in exchange for art loans, special exhibitions, and the right to attach the Louvre's name to a new museum. The Louvre Abu Dhabi is part of a massive cultural and tourist development on a still entirely undeveloped island, Saadiyat Island.[67] The joint-venture exemplifies how cultural assets that have been hereto assumed to be rooted become mobile and detached from their original location.

More importantly, however, the Louvre Abu Dhabi illustrates how a 'distant' cultural good and brand are used to build and profile a so far 'non-existent' location, here sandwiched between desert and the shallow waters of the Persian Gulf. The Louvre, an iconic 'old world' institution, has sold its brand to a country that was non-existent some thirty years ago. Indeed, one day more tourists may be attracted to visit part of the Louvre's collection in Abu Dhabi rather than in Paris – to the extent that Abu Dhabi could well foster Paris' global brand value, one day.

However, the most prolific example of how location assumes a pivotal role in a 'flat' world is international finance. Capital markets have been at the forefront of deconstructing national borders and as a result have served as a showcase of a borderless world. But it appears that location increasingly matters more rather than less in global finance, too. And the respective policy responses to the current credit crisis will reinforce this phenomenon. The pre-eminent role the London Stock Exchange has assumed amongst foreign issuers is insightful. In 2007, the London Stock Exchange raised US$30bn on behalf of foreign issuers, double the amount raised by non-US companies on the New York Stock Exchange and NASDAQ combined. This trend is unlikely to revert in the short-term, despite the credit crisis.

Against this drift, New York's Mayor Michael Bloomberg commissioned a McKinsey report that was published with alarming conclusions in spring 2007.[68] An excessively litigious environment and burdensome regulations, such as Sarbanes-Oxley,[69] were primarily held responsible for the deteriorating attractiveness of New York as a destination for public market listings. Both factors have undoubtedly increased costs to a level where the competitiveness of the US as a listing venue is compromised. And fewer companies, both foreign as well as American, will decide to list on US exchanges.

A too often ignored consideration determining Wall Street's overall competitiveness, however, is America's tax system. The US's extraterritorial tax system, empowering its authorities to tax – on a worldwide basis – not only US citizens' but foreign US residents' income and capital gains, effectively shelters America from full economic competition. It will compromise the US's ability to attract foreign wealth, in particular in a world where the economic epicenter has not only shifted eastwards but when the US does not necessarily represent any longer the most vibrant system and place altogether – at least in the near future.

In a flattening and mobile world, a country's ability to attract foreign wealth will increasingly determine economic competitive advantage. And it is a country's fiscal model – from provisioning and financing public services to overall taxation – that will increasingly drive an individual's choice for domicile and residence. Were US citizens and foreign US residents not taxed on a world-wide basis, competition amongst tax systems around the world would increase. More and more Americans would consider residency offshore while the rest of the world would compete – by way of a competitive tax system – to capture most of Americans' spending power. America, consequently, would be challenged to attract foreign capital inflows through a reformed tax system, too.

Low or preferential taxation of foreigners is essential to attract expertise and wealth from abroad. As the individual's global mobility is rising, the tax systems of the US and Europe can no longer rely upon the outdated notion that their economies exercise a form of magnetism on global capital flows or, for that matter, their own citizens. We are at the beginning of a new era in politics where a country's competitiveness to keep and attract the brightest and the wealthiest from around the world will have to redefine the domestic political agenda. In fact, the individual is emerging as the power broker amongst leading economies.

In no small measure, Britain's economic success, outpacing that of Germany since the fall of the Berlin Wall, is in particular due to the favorable tax status granted to foreigners that are resident but non-domiciled in the UK. Effectively, foreigners' capital gains are non-taxable as long as they are generated abroad, not repatriated to the UK and – since the changes introduced in the 2008 budget – a *club membership* fee of GBP 30,000 is paid.

This two-tier tax system has turned the UK into one of the world's biggest offshore banking markets attracting new wealth from China, Russia, India and the Middle East to make London – despite its rainy weather – rather than New York their residence of choice. It is the wealth of those individuals combined with the battalions of bankers and lawyers from around the world catering to that wealth, which have allowed London to overtake New York as the world's leading banking market. Undoubtedly, the UK's principles-based and above-politics approach to financial markets regulations, too, has been critical to making London the world's preferred destination for a company's public market listing.

Britain's economy is not short of red tapes. But its success in financial markets is largely due to the Englishman's understanding that whatever attracts trade, investment and foreign wealth is good for the country. If it requires favorable taxation, then so be it. The world should more carefully study Britain's success in finance and banking – despite any clouds that the current credit crisis may temporarily cast. It is no surprise that it is Great Britain that has been a major force of influence throughout the history of Dubai. A favorable tax treatment granted to the world's entrepreneurs and traders to attract their wealth has been a trademark of Dubai's development since the 19th century. The success of any economy – and the financial sector most potently highlights any shortcomings – is dependent on its ability to open itself favorably to the rest of the world.

While the British do so by instinct, Americans have too often displayed fear-driven protectionist reflexes. In particular, since September 11, 2001, the US has become a more introverted country with mountains, sometimes, fencing off its borders. And emerging places like Dubai and Abu Dhabi, independent of their respective size and location, will more and more drive competition amongst economic systems by way of their sheer openness, as Singapore and Hong Kong have done for many decades. The world is flat, but the 'flattening' free flow of capital and people will paradoxically re-emphasize the importance of location, as re-location is a real and attractive option.

Today, in the face of the erosion of local roots, the individual is challenged – more than ever – to think and act. Opportunities for professional self-fulfillment are no longer there to take or leave, but must be conquered and reaffirmed every day. The ability to think and move beyond national and cultural boundaries will be the individual's most potent navigation tool. And the ongoing credit crisis will put to the test an increasing number of individuals – in particular those bankers whose swaggering self-identity was largely based on the deceptive belief that they are the very force of globalization. Indeed, it will be interesting to watch how the many Bear Stearns and Lehman Brothers bankers will reinvent themselves in a shrinking financial services industry without fundamentally questioning their destiny in the absence of reconsidering location.

A country's ability to create jobs, facilitate entrepreneurial risk-taking and guarantee economic – not a priori, political – liberties without the costs of an overburdening and public services-poor state will increasingly determine an individual's choice of residence. In particular since the fall of the Berlin Wall, Great Britain – one of the least evil and most mature liberal systems of the world – was a major beneficiary of Continental Europe's brain drain as the leadership of Germany and France put pan-European political institution-building ahead of economic growth and job creation. The *mobile* left for places such as London and Dubai.

But Britain's competitive advantage cannot be taken for granted. Regressions are frequent. The suspicion that recent changes to Britain's preferential tax treatment of foreigners may just be the start of far-reaching limitations to the offshore-ability of certain assets and capital gains combined with a credit-crisis stricken financial sector will suggest to many expatriates that it is time to *Exit* and move on to places that define the next stage of personal advancement.

During the past five to ten years, Dubai has increasingly emerged as one of the preferred destinations for the world's mobile to fulfill their ambitions. As much as the United States benefited once from the discontent of large parts of Europe's population, Dubai's growth is directly linked to the desire of a growing number of individuals to *Exit* their home countries in search for a brighter future abroad. The fact that Dubai only attracts a small portion – in terms of numbers – is irrelevant. But undeniably Dubai is the most prolific microcosm of this trend. Location matters. And the number of locations on offer will increase. *Who's your City?*

The Future of the West: A Question of Being

When Oswald Spengler, a high-school teacher in Munich, published the first edition of his bestselling *The Decline of the West* in the summer of 1918, he was considered a pessimist. He had a tendency to exaggerate. But, today, maybe more than ever, his work appears to be of vital relevance to better understand the West's present predicament and changing self-identity. In fact, as the world's capitalistic epicenter shifts eastwards, will the West finally become a dead concept deprived of any meaning beyond its historic relevance? And does it really matter?

The "decline of the West", Spengler writes, "which at first sight may appear, like the corresponding decline of the Classical Culture, a phenomenon limited in time and space, we now perceive to be a philosophical problem that, when comprehended in all its gravity, includes within itself every great question of Being."[70] For Spengler, the phenomenon of the decline or fallibility of the West was less of a gloomy projection than a potent tool to nourish a sense of history, sharpen self-awareness and understand how much we corrupted the very values and traditions that made us strong in the first place.

The historian Mark Mazower summarized it perfectly for Europeans, but it equally applies to Americans: "If the west turns out to have been an idea that shielded Europeans from the consciousness of their own decline, the disappearance of the west may not be a bad thing."[71] We remain trapped in an identity of Western self-righteousness and superiority. If it wasn't for the economic awakening of powerhouses like China, we would hardly dare to question the competitiveness of our political choices and economic structures.

In fact, China's international ascent emerges as the closest and most credible challenger to the US's global economic supremacy. However, China's legacy is likely to dent a linear path to ascension. Demographic trends, uncontrolled urban development, environmentally disastrous infrastructure projects, and contaminated products from toys to food – against a background of increasing popular unrest and a morally and ideologically crippled Communist Party – are likely to challenge China's future superpower status. For now, though, the world must learn to contend with China as a disruptive force.

While China, amongst others, is unfailingly shifting the world's epicenter eastwards, Pax Americana is likely to remain the dominant world order, despite all gloomy projections and a battery of costly US policies since the turn of the century. The United States is too big a market, too capitalistic a system and still too energetic and youthful in spirit, not to remain the world's leading nation – at least for foreseeable generations. But America and the West are in need of a *New Frontier* experience.

"The first three hundred years of American history is the story of a society developing along a moving frontier."[72] At the heart of understanding America, is the westward movement, the "spearhead of a dynamic society forever moving into new horizons of untapped opportunities."[73] In fact, America's frontier experience is the world's truly inspiring force that Dubai has come so close to revive in the last decade – despite questions around Dubai's substance and sustainability.

When in 1890 the Census Bureau of the United States officially announced the closing of the frontier[74], for a moment, it appeared as history was coming to an end. What next? A nation whose character was not only shaped by the abundance of space and natural resources but a forward-moving dynamism, could no longer equate physical movement with advancement towards untapped opportunities.

Fredrick Jackson Turner's 1893 publication of "The Significance of the Frontier in American History"[75] captures the fears at the time. The future of American democracy, passion for new ventures and pioneering individualism, all nurtured by the frontier experience, were under threat. Turner's articles, representative of his time, were "filled with anxiety that the American ideology might die out."[76] For Turner, the frontier experience was more metaphysical than physical. He was calling for a renaissance of this forward-moving spirit.

America had to supply itself with a "New West", a new frontier. Following the Great War, in 1920, Guy Emerson, an attorney-banker, published *The New Frontier*.[77] Business initiatives rather than new land should be the new frontier.[78] The confusion, contradictions and aspirations generated by the frontier debate have transpired throughout America's modern history. The end of the frontier, inevitably, had a lasting impact on America's self-identity and, subsequently, its engagement with the rest of the world.

At times, America appears to be still trapped by the Census Bureau announcement of 1890, and the threat the latter allegedly posed to the longevity of the American ideology of progress. Categorical patriotism turned into a question of being and defined electoral campaigns based on simplicities such as *for us vs. against us* into winning strategies In fact, in the US, *Voice* is only accepted within certain and tacitly defined boundaries. Anything beyond those boundaries is suspicious of being possibly unpatriotic, un-American, and jeopardizing the longevity of Americaness.

But America's sheer energy and passion for the New Frontier, as Emerson had defined it, have made the United States unique, to the present day. Its tireless capability to reinvent itself stands in stark contrast to Europe's inability to reform and reinvigorate itself. "Whereas the classical European struggle occurred between the "haves" and the "have nots", the battle in the United States involved the "haves" and the "will haves".[79] Despite an increasing polarization of America's wealth-creation, the *American Dream* has not died. And Americans truly love their country.

In important aspects, Dubai partially embodies the re-naissance of America's early 20th century *New Frontier* spirit: "poly-ethnic, multi-racial, openly materialistic, and self-consciously individualistic"[80], embracing "free enterprise and change as basic values."[81] However, with two qualifications: the absence in Dubai of anxiety and resourcefulness that have been so characteristic of the American experience.

America's Puritan legacy, eager "to reconcile much-needed individualism with the fear it might promote anarchy"[82] and to implement "a set of rituals of anxiety that could at once encourage and control the energies of free enterprise"[83] is substituted in Dubai by a cocktail of moderate Islam[84] and hereditary authoritarianism. The absence of plenty in Dubai, best exemplified by scarce oil resources and limited land, proved to be Dubai's blessing, empowering a series of visionary rulers to not only constantly reinvent their city but to strive for the ultimate.

The question of the longevity of the West, central to Spengler's concerns, has become irrelevant. The days of the concept of the West are numbered. It is no longer a question of geography or politics. It is a question of being – consciously being part of a growing and changing world. It would have been beyond the wildest imaginations of Oswald Spengler that an unknown camel-populated fishing village on the borders of the Persian Gulf will one day become one of the world's most decadent champions of free enterprise and free movement, two core values of Western civilization.

معا نبني مستقبل دبي

Building the future of Dubai

We apologise for the inconvenience
during the upgrade of roads. For any
queries please Contact

Part II: 'The City Where the Future Starts': Contours of Dubai⁸⁵

"A searing blast of heat greeted Fitz as he walked out of the Iran Air jet at Dubai's new international airport. To his delight he found Ibrahim Matroos, resplendent in white kandura, his kuffiyah held in place by the agahal, a double-strand black camel rope, waiting for him at the bottom of the plane's steps. Ibrahim was one of Rashid's important courtiers...

"You have chosen the evil time of the beginning of the heat to come, I am sorry", Ibrahim apologized. From June to September the temperature averages 120 degrees, sometimes dropping to 100 at night. The humidity reaches nearly 100 percent. Most activity was at a standstill and the European community left the Arabian Gulf area during the summer...

It was a short drive along the Creek to Sepah's home. "Sepah's father, Yousef, was one of the largest pearl merchants in the Gulf", Ibrahim explained. "Then after your great war the Japanese flooded the market with their cultured pearls and that was the end of the Arabian Gulf natural-pearl trade. Yousef finally went back to his native Persia to live out his days, but Sepah and the Ruler had become almost like brothers. Rashid convinced Sepah he should stay in Dubai and help build up the Creek as a great international port..."

Dubai's becoming the world's biggest boom town. It all depends on how much risk you want to take with your money. Put it into gold smuggling and you can triple it in one smuggling season. Of course, you take a risk, but what they do there is put a syndicate together and then make four trips to India. If three out of four trips are successful the profits run ever larger...

At least half the Ten Tola Bar business consisted of Arab men who, true to their customs, never took women out but were glad to see Western girls at the places they went. Only in this one place throughout the Arabian Gulf could such an establishment exist. Dubai was the supreme monument to free enterprise and it was the Ruler's excellent business judgment that made Dubai the most important Arab port on the Gulf. Dubai had achieved impressive wealth before oil had been found. Now there was no limit to the commercial heights this small emirate could achieve."

Robin Moore, *Dubai* (1976)

Introduction: Historical Roots of the World's New Microcosm

"The Golden Age, which a blind tradition has hitherto placed in the past, is ahead of us."

Saint-Simon (1825)

The birth of modern Dubai is best traced to 1833 when the Maktoum family, a discontented faction of Abu Dhabi's ruling elite, split off and seized control of Dubai. Ever since, the Maktoum family has controlled Dubai. "This marked the start of Dubai's ascendancy. Thus, too, was born the uneasy bond between Dubai and Abu Dhabi."[86]

Tension between the two sheikdoms over borders culminated in a war lasting from 1945 to 1948. It was a light war with hardly any human casualties, but nonetheless it documented tension. A tension, that has been of less relevance during the past thirty years when Abu Dhabi's oil wealth partly subsidized Dubai's development. While competition may very well be on the rise today as Abu Dhabi diversifies its oil-centric economy into areas such as tourism where Dubai has long assumed a leadership position, the fortunes of Dubai and Abu Dhabi remain intractably interwoven.

Already in the early stages of the Maktoum family's leadership in the 19th century, Dubai, "split by a 14km-long creek which led into a natural harbor, established itself as a flourishing hub for re-export trade. Other Gulf ports along the Persian coast could not compete. Traders preferred Dubai's liberal policies – especially its lower taxes on foreigners."[87] But Dubai's economic wealth remained modest as a 1908 record summarizes it as including "4,000 date trees, 1,650 camels, 45 horses, 380 donkeys, 430 cattle and 960 goats. In the Creek, there are 155 boats for diving and trading and 20 small boats to take passengers between the two banks of the Creek".[88]

Dubai developed a particular expertise in boatbuilding. And boats were critical to Dubai's economy as the principal source of foreign currency was derived from the pearl trade as well as Dubai's souqs, the biggest trading place in the Persian Gulf. Pearling had been the foundation of Dubai's economy for hundreds of years, reaching maximum economic output at the beginning of the twentieth century.

"With increasing wealth and a demand for rich, rather than gaudy or showy jewellery such as diamonds, no gem commanded better market prices than the pearl."[89] Two events, however, dramatically changed the prospects of the natural pearl trade. The 1929 crash on Wall Street pulled the United States, and consequently other parts of the world, into a severe economic depression. Demand for luxury goods, in particular pearls, died overnight.

More importantly, however, future demand for Dubai's natural pearls was killed by Japan's Kokichi Mikimoto who discovered the secret of pearl culturing. Japan's cultured pearls started swamping global markets and substituted demand for natural pearls with a surging demand for cultured pearls. The "effect was catastrophic and immediate, not only for local pearling merchants, but for the entire community. This was an industry built on borrowing."[90]

As with any economic activity built upon a high-level of borrowing, the sensitivity to any changes in demand and supply can easily put survival at stake. As "Dubai was a regional hub of this booming industry"[91] and pearling constituted the backbone of its local economy, Dubai's future as the Gulf's leading trading center was not only challenged but close to non-existent following the collapse in pearl trade. Unemployment, the absence of exports and hard currency, and a shortage of food supplies plunged a small but relatively well-off trading town, encircled by desert and sea, into a crisis of unimaginable proportions.

At this point, Dubai was in need of nothing more but visionary leadership to reinvent a bankrupt economy. It is during this moment of severe crisis that the spirit of Dubai, as we now know it, was born. It is at this juncture that Dubai's history as a modern force of capitalism truly started. It was also the birth of the leadership of Sheikh Rashid bin Saeed Al Maktoum (1912-1990), who made "daring to think the unthinkable" the trademark of Dubai's capitalistic way.

While authoritarian leadership of the Maktoum family, characterized by visionary long-term growth plans, is the foundation of Dubai's success, external events and influences have critically determined Dubai's course of history. Great Britain's influence and the challenge of constant economic reinvention in the face of limited natural resources paired with the overall high level of dependency upon the outside world in terms of labor, entrepreneurs, natural resources and markets stand out as Dubai's most potent historical forces.

Since the 19th century, Dubai's historic laxity in taxation was a primary force to attract entrepreneurs, in particular from Iran and India, to set up trading operations in Dubai. It is that laxity that forms today the basis of Dubai's free zone growth areas, attracting more and more entrepreneurial-minded individuals, partly, from excessively regulated and overtaxed countries.

Dubai's exceptionally hot and humid climate, during the best part of the year, and the absence of oil discoveries until the mid-20th century have

more or less put off invaders. "The arrival of the Portuguese as the first distant power to dominate certain parts of the Gulf and Oman completely transformed the regional power structure from the beginning of the 16th century"[92] as a disconnected and fragmented tribal population had to define a self-identity vis-à-vis a foreign Third Party. But the Portuguese "were expelled from all the Arab and Persian ports by the middle of the 17th century, and they left no religious and hardly any cultural imprint, except for their cannons and the ruined forts of their garrisons."[93]

But Dubai's geographic position in the Persian Gulf placed it at the center of Great Britain's global trading interests. Consequently, Britain assumed, though never as a colonizer, a pivotal and lasting role in Dubai's internal affairs until well after the birth of the United Arab Emirates in 1971.[94] Britain's primary concern to protect its global trading interests as well as its maritime supremacy vis-à-vis rivaling European powers formidably matched Dubai's innate trading culture and provided security as well as stability, paramount to Dubai's economic growth.

Britain's influence can be best summarized in the words of Lord George Curzon, the Viceroy of India, when his Royal Navy sloop anchored off the coast of Sharjah, the UAE's third-largest emirate, in 1903. "We were here before any other power, in modern times, had shown its face in these waters. We found strife and we created order. It was our commerce as well as your security that was threatened and called for protection. We saved you from extinction at the hands of your neighbours. We opened these seas to the ships of all nations, and enabled their flags to fly in peace."[95]

While Britain never colonized the Gulf, the English were sensitive to controlling the region's political as well as economic development. Lord Curzon's words eloquently summarize the position: "We have not seized or held your territory, have not destroyed your independence but have preserved it. The peace of these waters must still be maintained. Your independence will continue to be upheld and in this the influence of the British government must remain supreme. The British government has no desire to interfere, and have never interfered in your internal affairs, provided that the Chiefs govern their territories with justice, and respect the rights of the foreign traders residing therein."[96]

Great Britain pursued a minimalist approach focusing on what was necessary to provide stability, allow trade to flourish, and to keep rival European powers at bay, in particular when it came to maritime trading routes. Britain was sensitive to local structures and customs as its interests were capitalistic in nature rather than ideological. It certainly was not concerned with building democratic institutions or championing a campaign of Western-style liberties.

It is primarily that approach, best characterized by pragmatism, mercantilism, and the pursuit of stability – the latter usually through diplomacy – that allowed Britain to build and maintain an empire over several centuries. Today's ideological obsession with democracy and liberty, irrespective of history, culture and circumstances of a particular place – an obsession best displayed by the United States' foreign policy – presents a drastic contrast to the traditional British approach practiced in the Persian Gulf.

Europe's accelerating process of industrialization and the unionized concern for workers' rights and benefits resulted in the birth of the modern welfare state across Europe at the end of the 19th century. And it was the combination of a changing global political climate together with the fiscal burden of the welfare state – in particular amid a severe economic recession across Europe – which was partly responsible for the fall of the British Empire and ultimately mandated the complete withdrawal of British forces from the Gulf in 1971. But Great Britain's legacy remains noticeable to the present day. Economic growth and overall prosperity is certainly higher in Britain's rather than France's former colonies.

Once the British withdrawal from the Gulf was in sight, the rulers of the seven emirates endorsed the concept of the Federation of the United Arab Emirates, which was formalized on December 2, 1971. Thanks to the 1970s' oil-shocks, substantial revenues financed compulsory free education, the opening of the first university in 1978, rapid and widespread implementation of infrastructure projects and substantial improvements in health services, early-on. Jebel Ali Free Zone, one of the first free zones in the Gulf region, opened in 1985. It has been fundamental to Dubai's growth strategy.

Ever since, Dubai has been on a trajectory of economic development that, measured over time, remains unmatched by any one country. Vision, determination and uncompromising faith in the future form the basis of Dubai's success. And one single family largely deserves the credit. But as is true for any tribal society, the leadership of a particular family is subject to challenge. And the Maktoum family has been no exception.

Throughout the 19th century as well as good parts of the 20th century the Maktoum family's authority was hugely dependent on British support. And more importantly, following the creation of the United Arab Emirates, any potential discontent was appeased with an elaborate system of wealth distribution "in which all members of the national population, even recently urbanized bedouin, were provided with housing, jobs, education and welfare."[97]

It is this welfare system that continues to serve as an important foundation for *Loyalty* to the Maktoum family. But it comes at the price of a national population that is largely unemployable due to its over-reliance on welfare benefits reaching as far into the private lives as financial contributions towards weddings. Today, Dubai's challenge is to reintegrate those nationals – which in total constitute a minority of no more than ten percent – into the super-competitive and super-global Dubai economy, dominated by expatriates.

As late as the 1970s, when air-conditioning was a rarity and a road system was hardly existent, Robin Moore wrote his visionary novel 'Dubai'. Then, few dared to predict modern Dubai's meteoric rise.

Hatred for Limits

> "We were in a race against time and we won...
> ...the race has only just begun."
>
> Sheikh Mohammad al Maktoum, Ruler of Dubai (2007)[98]

It is Dubai's face of relentless change and continuous reinvention in search for new limits that not only has come to define it but energizes and attracts an increasing number of foreigners. If modernity is defined as this "one continuous, unstoppable and fast accelerating effort"[99] where 'your own limitations are the only limitations', then Dubai is the ultimate embodiment of modernity.

There is no legacy to protect, and there is no future to debate. There is a complete absence of public discourse. The media are, at best, informative, but not challenging. The indigenous culture and local population are close to non-existent in light of expatriates' dominance. This is a world without politics. Dubai is one big enterprise led by a strong and capable management board determined to do whatever protects its power base while fostering economic advancement.

The street life is sterile and impersonal. A minimum of Islamic values preserves social peace and safety without compromising the pleasure-centric lifestyle of Western tourism and expatriatism. But for now Dubai has become a physical as well as metaphysical home for like-minded individuals and enterprises that have exited their native countries – countries where politics, lack of opportunity and high taxes often suffocate agility and motivation.

Construction best displays Dubai's ambitions. More than 20% of the world's construction cranes are working around the clock in Dubai.[100] And the skyline keeps changing rapidly. Dubai is one large construction site. Any city map is likely to be outdated by the time it goes to print. In July 2007, Burj Dubai has become the world's tallest building as its construction height passed 512.1 meters.[101] The targeted height remains a secret to keep potential competitors guessing.

Burj Dubai is destined to give the Middle East again the honor of hosting the earth's tallest structure, after the Eiffel Tower upset in 1889 the 43-century reign of Egypt's Great Pyramid of Giza.[102] Dubai will not wait for any other city to challenge Burj Dubai's status. It is expected that Dubai's Al-Burj with a minimal height of 750 meters and to be completed by 2010 will rival Burj Dubai for the world's tallest building title. Effectively, the world's two tallest buildings will be in Dubai. But rumors about potential challengers in the Middle East are on the rise. The current credit crisis, though, will undoubtedly mandate a review of ongoing construction projects.

It is difficult to capture the magnitude of Dubai's development without the historical perspective. "The first house built of concrete blocks was constructed in 1956. A large number of inhabitants of Dubai lived in palm-frond (barasti) houses until well into the 1960s."[103] The Palm Islands construction, a giant property development built into the sea, is the first man-made project to be visible from space ever, or, since the Great Wall of China. Dubai was non-existent on the global aviation map until the 1980s. By 2010, Dubai is expected to operate the world's largest airport, in terms of both cargo and passengers.

Dubailand, a massive leisure and tourist attraction spread over 3 billion square feet and scheduled to be completed in 2009, will be approximately four and a half times the size of Manhattan, and, symbolically, complete with an Eiffel Tower. It will also feature 'Dubai Sunny Mountain Ski dome', an all-year winter skiing experience – in the middle of the desert. The project consists of the world's largest dome including a giant revolving ski slope and a cable-lift, going through and around an artificial mountain range. A penguinarium and polar bears will add an "Arctic Experience". A deluxe hotel and a shopping mall, as is typical for most of Dubai's developments, are part of the package.

Entertainment attractions are critical to expanding Dubai's tourism industry. But Dubai attempts to be more than amusement-driven tourism. One would hardly associate with Dubai one of the world's largest single site aluminum smelters. The 76,000-plus ton capacity primary aluminum smelter is part of Dubal, Dubai's industrial flagship. Industrialization will play an important part of Dubai's future development, as the objective remains to increase exports rather than just re-exports as part of the growing non-oil related trade. We are largely still dealing with a "superficially successful post-oil economy."[104] And Dubai remains in a race against time. This time the objective is not just diversification, but to make Dubai's economic fortunes less dependent on foreigners' will and interest to invest.

Dubai's visionary planning is largely centered on the knowledge economy. Education is a central theme of Dubai's economic strategy. Surprisingly to many Western observers, women form the majority of the output of UAE universities. Healthcare City, a partnership with Harvard Medical School, is set up to turn Dubai into one of the world's leading medical centers in research, education and practice. Healthcare is free and accessible for all residents in Dubai. Internet City, Media City and Dubai International Financial Center (DIFC), respectively, are other prominent clusters, or tax-free zones, attracting leading services and financial firms from around the world. Often, though, the grandiose branding of those initiatives falls short

of substance to match the ambition. But filling that gap may just be a matter of time.

The DIFC, despite Dubai's liquidity-poor securities exchanges, has rapidly emerged as the leading hub for international investment banks' Middle Eastern operations, in particular to advise the region's sovereign wealth funds. During the past twelve months some of the banks' most senior executives in London and New York have been transferred to Dubai. The seniority of the bankers is an attribute to the force Dubai has become as a financial gateway to the Middle East.

In Islamic finance, one of the world's fastest growing banking sectors, Dubai is benchmarking itself against Kuala Lumpur, the market leader. More importantly, Dubai has copied the UK Financial Services Authority's principles-based financial markets regulation. In fact, former employees of the FSA play an active role within the DIFC. Engaging the best possible external expertise has been a critical ingredient of Dubai's success.

Dubai's success is not the by-product of petrodollars.[105] In fact, the absence of significant oil resources forced the city-state to play against time and invent in a relatively short period of time a diversified economy across a multitude of sectors in services, technology, engineering, retail and finance. Today, non-oil gross domestic product amounts to approximately 94 percent![106] The question remains: how sustainable is it?

The key to understanding Dubai's success is that infrastructure investments have always been the primary focus. When the late Ruler Sheik Rashid decided to deepen the Creek and build a world-class container port in the 1960s, the business was not there. "Build the infrastructure and they will come" has been Dubai's credo, since the early days. Today, Dubai's port infrastructure is competing head-to-head with Singapore and Rotterdam. And Dubai Ports World (DP World) has emerged as one of the world's leading ports operator.

Decisive for Dubai's massive infrastructure development is the public-private partnership model. Contrary to common assertions, it is often international private and sovereign capital rather than domestic Government funds that assume a leading role in Dubai's development. For everything that is planned and executed in Dubai, there is one overriding objective: to make money and strive for the very best. While the Ruler of Dubai is the master developer, it is private expertise and entrepreneurship that drives the city. Dubai provides the stage, best summarized by business-friendly regulation with Western-style protection of property rights. Foreigners are invited to invest and 'play the game'.

In addition to world-class expertise, risk-diversification is fundamental to the 'Dubai way'. Already in the early days when Dubai's principal economic activity was pearl diving, expeditions where syndicated amongst many traders to spread risk. During the past years, economic diversification has been taken to a new level. A spree of international acquisitions of assets in real estate, retail, infrastructure and financial services has significantly diversified Dubai's stake in the global economy.[107] It is at this juncture that large parts of the West, in particular the US, start meeting Dubai.

Governments across the world, primarily in the US and Europe, are increasingly alarmed by the pace at which state-controlled funds are taking important stakes in flagship Western companies. Imposing controls on so-called 'sovereign wealth funds' is not only high on the agenda of Western lawmakers[108] but is another reflex of democracies' political apparatus that is fearful of losing control. National security considerations have become democracies' 21st century Trojan horse to increase the state's political powers. Demand for a national security review was Washington's immediate response to the September 2007 announcement of Dubai taking a 19.9% stake in NASDAQ, the US' second largest stock exchange.

The trail of global acquisitions is just starting and is by no means limited to the West. The Middle East and Africa are key target areas, too. For now, Dubai's international acquisitions appear to be financially rather than politically motivated. Capital gains are realized opportunistically as trades in Daimler Chrysler and Madame Tussauds Group demonstrated.[109] But Dubai's overall engagement with the rest of the world is on the rise.

Dubai's growth, though, has been neither without troubles nor contradictions and shortcomings. While Dubai's mission is centered on continuous improvement, there is no time to coordinate, and there is little time to learn from mistakes. Today's super-charged growth is likely to create tomorrow's legacy.

Urban planning is mostly non-existent. Dubai is a patch of property developments that do not necessarily form a coherent whole. The architecture is mediocre. Dubai's façade is largely that of naked capitalism: mirrored glass. The absence of pavements is testimony to the automobile's dominant position. Any remaining public space is constantly threatened by celebrity-branded property developments.[110]

One of Dubai's biggest challenges is to address the city's mounting traffic congestion. With a population expected to grow at more than 6% annually from approximately 1.4 million in 2006 to reach more than 3 million by 2017, and a target to serve 15 million tourists per year by 2010,[111] public transport is a main concern. Dubai Metro, a driverless, fully automated light rail network, is under construction and expected to be completed in 2009.

Certain aspects of Dubai's shortcomings, though, sometimes appear to bear the colors of a pre-Victorian slave trade. According to Human Rights Watch, the international non-governmental human rights organization, the violation of labor laws has been widespread. Unpaid salaries[112] and abusive working as well as living conditions have caused revolt[113] amongst workers. Overambitious construction projects have compromised safety measures leading to deaths in certain cases.[114]

Dubai's constructions are 24-hour operations, mainly staffed by illiterate South Asian and Sub-continental migrant workers, housed in specially-built labor camps that often fall short of basic sanitary hygiene[115]. Suicide is not uncommon.[116] A construction worker's testimony lends weight to the reality of Dubai's dark side, in particular when considering that his salary is tenfold of what he can make in native India: "I heard a lot of things about Dubai, how great it was. But when I came here I hated it. I do not ever want to come back here."[117]

The most prolific case of abuse and human trafficking, though, directly implicates Dubai's current Ruler. A lawsuit filed in Miami[118] in September 2006 on behalf of some ten thousand migrant children and their families requesting unspecified damages, accuses Sheikh Muhammad bin Rashid Al Maktoum of enslaving and forcing young boys to work under brutal conditions as camel racing jockeys[119] over the past three decades.[120] In the long-run, the lawsuits will be nothing more but a footnote in history.

Dubai is trying to accomplish in several decades what some of the world's leading cities have gradually achieved over hundreds of years. It is a race

against time. Shortcomings, contradictions and abuses are typical for the 'transitional' stages of urban growth. Nothing justifies the abuses and shortcomings. But the government of Dubai must be credited with addressing the wrongdoings with the best intentions and determination.[121]

Dubai's latest aggressive push to turn the city into a commerce-driven hub in global contemporary and Islamic art, largely orchestrated by the Dubai International Financial Center, not only reflects the nexus of arts and money, but is partly a response to the silent cry for the content that nourishes mind and soul. Dubai's initiatives, though, will fail in the long-term unless profitability considerations are abandoned and the City sponsors a native platform for a diverse cultural scene across all media, supported with educational institutions. Whether Dubai's activist pursuit of building Islamic art collections will foster a more profiled Dubai-Emirati self-identity, remains to be seen, too.

But despite all shortcomings, Dubai, for now, serves as a microcosm that fills the vacuum that the West has left vacant: the empowerment of the individual to master one's destiny and advancement in pursuit of prosperity and self-fulfillment. Dubai's low-tax environment and the absence of trade and capital controls are critical. Dubai's primary focus is to provide the optimal legal and regulatory framework to promote entrepreneurship and wealth creation. So far, few Emirati nationals are part of this carefully engineered stage, and there is a pressuring mandate to integrate into this expatriate-dominated economy those Emirati nationals that appear to be trapped in some government-inflicted complacency fueled by rich and far-reaching welfare benefits.

There is no doubt that the visionary planning of Dubai's successive Rulers has created something new – beyond Singapore and Hong Kong. While the economic models of Hong Kong and Singapore have been largely built on the pledge of political stability and minimal trade and capital controls, Dubai's survival required more. The combination of a competitive re-export port infrastructure, Western tourism and extensive sports entertainment – Singapore is just starting to catch up on the latter with Formula One – allowed Dubai to emerge as the world's gateway to the Middle East and beyond.

The "idea that human beings can replace the world-that-is with another and different world, entirely of their own making was almost wholly absent from human thought before the advent of modern times."[122] Dubai has taken modernity to new heights as it demonstrates that independent of size, in the absence of natural resources and even when situated in a politically and economically troubled region, there is no obstacle to building a force of prosperity that can attract the rest of the world.

Dubai's spirit is based on a hatred for limits. It is this hatred that has allowed Dubai to achieve the unthinkable. It is this hatred that attracts and inspires more and more people from around the world. They all may not entirely agree with everything in Dubai. And they may very well question the sustainability of a yet to be proven economic microcosm. But they are all taken by a sense of positive energy in their drive for achievement. It is a feeling that, for many, has been non-existent in the Western world for some time.

But it is this hatred for limits – in particular, in the absence of both humility and prudence – that could well be the unmaking of Dubai, too. This spirit of limitlessness is now largely held responsible for the demise of the Western financial system. The portrait of a card house falling apart

is hard to dismiss. But the very timing of the global credit crisis – as much as it represents a risk to Dubai's growth and overall sustainability – embeds also a unique opportunity to partly demonstrate the resilience of Dubai's system and to implement changes to avert the worst possible crisis.

Dubai's authoritarian governance model – contrary to Western democracy – is better positioned[123] to avoid the trap of glorifying the mantra of more regulation as the answer to all ills. Perhaps at no other juncture in the modern history of Dubai than today, is the visionary leadership of the Maktoum family as critical to the city's future.

Freedom, or at least the sense of it, always comes at a price. Paradoxically, it is often a feeling of oppressiveness that, in turn, fuels the desire for more freedom. It is a self-feeding process that, over time, has corrupted the meaning of freedom. And there is no lasting happiness and appreciation for freedom in the absence of duty. An individual's and, for that matter, a society's survival and competitiveness is dependent on the individual's civic engagement. In the long run, each individual, including the cosmopolitan nomad, will not escape – whether consciously or unconsciously – the desire to fulfill this basic need.

It is at this juncture where Dubai is likely to be most challenged. It is the Dubai paradox: while Dubai must strive for limitlessness to appeal to the rest of the world, it must construct a form of civic engagement that builds a responsible society, though, without challenging the Maktoum family's firm leadership of Dubai Inc.

Epilogue

"...the periods of creation, like the success of particular movements, occur when hope – the vision of Possibility – is vivid in many minds, when it is obvious to all that Construction is possible. Then the presence of obstacles and opposition is only another incentive to struggle. The uphill fight is going to be rewarded by an incomparable view from the summit. This was the feeling among the gifted at the height of the eighteenth century, and again in the great flowering of Romanticism and Liberalism. It sprang up once more after the fin de siècle lassitude as our own century began. The Cubist decade was a great producer of models. Then came the catastrophe of the Four Years' War of 1914-1918, which not only swept from the earth innumerable young geniuses, but showed the Western world that it could not protect civilization from its own stupid impulse. The spirit of the West has never really recovered from that shattering... The question now is whether the events we are witnessing are preparing another open and level ground for a reawakened animal faith and the creation of undreamed-of new things, or whether on the contrary our sullen doings have reached repetition in futility."

Jacques Barzun, *The Culture We Deserve (1989)*

My generation is longing for something 'new'. Dubai is new, but only to the extent that it has revived – and taken to the extreme – the long forgotten essence of the Western spirit: to celebrate a forward-looking advancement that defies established boundaries in time and space. Despite the absence of political rights, Dubai has created a sense of freedom, indeed EMANCIPATION – to dream and live the desire to achieve the improbable. It is a sense that America monopolized throughout the 20th century but that Western democracies, in particular in Europe, have been unable to instill amongst its populations for some time now. The question arises to what degree has Dubai fully exploited its freedom from history and culture, as America once did. "Did they go as far as they could?"[124]

Unless something truly new emerges from Dubai, the city's obsessive mercantilism paired with the dilemmas opposing self, society and a ruling gang will prove to be a potentially dangerous mix. In history, Dubai may be recorded as nothing more but another City of Desires, 'the soulless whore as a greedy automaton'.[125] But nonetheless, extremity – also in decadence – can be the antechamber of 'revolutions' in pursuit of the 'undreamed-of new'. Dubai is the ultimate embodiment of Western decadence. It is just a matter of time for its drive for limitlessness in construction and commerce to generate fatigue and boredom amongst the expatriate community that defines Dubai's face and economy. Whether the 'undreamed-of new' will eventually be born on Dubai's soil or not is irrelevant. For now, Dubai's historic contribution will be undeniable in at least three regards.

First, as a microcosm it has revived a *New Frontier* spirit that has not only served as a global magnet for *the mobile* but as an inspirational force empowering an entire generation of strategic economic development from Qatar and Abu Dhabi and reaching well beyond the Gulf. Consequently, Dubai has challenged the balance of power of the global capitalistic system. In fact, Dubai has played an uncontestable role in shifting the world's economic epicenter eastwards as well as re-validating the meaning of location in a supposedly *flat* world. Dubai has done so more impressively than China and India, though, on a smaller scale. In light of today's global credit crisis and the *toxic* consequences of aggressive leverage, one is understandably inclined to dismiss Dubai as one big bubble with deceivingly little substance. But despite all challenges, paradoxes and dilemmas, the credit crisis may turn out to advance Dubai's relative position within the global capitalistic system. The international standings of London as well as New York have been tarnished – at least temporarily. The current credit crisis will be an important juncture in the history of Dubai. The next steps will decisively shape history's verdict of this *fantastic* desert town.

Second, Dubai's unbounded mercantilist drive demonstrates in fast-forward that trade and investments as a pursuit for its own sake are likely to lead to futility. The quest for material wealth must be complemented by a cultural, spiritual and civic engagement. Dubai is now reaching that juncture where its future success will also be dependent upon its ability to satisfy - in addition to the pursuit of private wealth – human nature's basic needs for non-monetary nourishment. It is a juncture that will challenge, beyond Dubai, an entire generation. The rise in spirituality – independently of the brand of any particular religion – and the need for civic engagement, beyond democracy, are likely to shape the dawn of a new age. As much as Dubai may hold the key to progress, it may, at the end, become famous for

a disquieting warning shot that the wealth-pursuing and pleasure-centric Western life style, in the long-run, is doomed to turn against itself. Whether as a force of decadence or an inspiring guidepost, Dubai is likely to continue leaving its mark on the world.

Third and most importantly, Dubai's undeniable success to date – despite questions around its sustainability – has indirectly challenged the Western democratic governance model. A country's long-term economic prosperity is more and more dependent on openness, low and simplified taxation, and long-term infrastructure-centric growth plans based on public-private partnership models. Dubai, despite its authoritarian nature, can serve in many regards as an inspirational force for reforms of the Western governance model. This will be of particular relevance as the consequences of the credit crisis will impose far-reaching changes to the West's governance model.

As this book goes to print, leaders of the world's biggest developed and developing economies – the so-called Group-20, which was created after the emerging markets crisis a decade ago – are gathering in Washington for a summit that is increasingly branded as the beginning of 'Bretton Woods II' – alluding to the 1944 conference that took place in Bretton Woods under the leadership of John Maynard Keynes and created the World Bank and the International Monetary Fund as core pillars of today's global capitalistic system.

Independently of the outcome of any such summit, directives for more regulation and more institution-building are likely to define the global political scene for years to come. Leaders – across the G-20 - have been frustrated to witness the increasing erosion of their power and influence as markets took the lead during the past two decades. Politicians are now indulging in the fact that the balance of power is clearly shifting in favor of the state as the laissez-faire of the go-go market economy is discredited. Finance is inherently unstable. And, without question, the state has to play an important role to make it safer. But today's political leadership - filled with a desire to *make history*, for the sake of it - is ill-equipped.

In the minds of many Western leaders – probably more tacitly than explicitly – Dubai has been branded as the whore of the global capitalistic system sucking whatever it can get – Western cash and plenty of talented expatriates to perform the local act. And at a time when the world appears to be in search for substance and certainty, it may seem counterintuitive to look towards Dubai for an agenda to reignite sustainable growth. But certain elements that have determined Dubai's rapid economic development are what world leaders should dare to turn to, despite the *improbable* nature of the tasks.

To fundamentally over-haul the Western tax system by introducing low and standardized tax brackets for corporate and personal income and capital gains. Complete neutralization of off-shore tax heavens through competitiveness and magnetism. This is likely to reduce costly tax arbitrage and should allow resource re-allocation that is currently spent on tax mitigation and law enforcement. Such a measure, though, will threaten the survival of a significant part of democracies' bureaucratic apparatus as well as a sprawling accountancy, legal and tax services industry. Resistance from within the system will be overwhelming, and few politicians are prepared to risk their career. Tax reductions as an ad-hoc measure to stimulate the economy are futile in the long-term, as interests rates and taxes will have to rise eventually to finance a growing budget deficit. Tax reductions must be structural and part of a plan that emphasizes an important role for the private sector in public healthcare, transport and education.

To open the economy by gradually removing trade and capital barriers. There is a real risk that a global economic slowdown will revive protectionist sentiment and policies. The Doha round of trade talks appears to have failed. The G-20 should commit to a fresh fast-track global trade round of tariff reductions leveraging the existing credit crisis. A more open economy is more likely to generate sustainable economic growth. No country is to gain from trade protectionism. However, previous trade rounds to lower tariffs have failed for a reason: lobbyists will try to hijack the process, and usually they succeed.

To launch country-specific public infrastructure funds managed and largely capitalized by the private sector. Infrastructure investments will represent democracies' biggest challenge going forward.[126] Sustainably competitive public transport, health and education systems require enormous amounts of capital that governments cannot finance on their own in the long-run. The private sector must play a pivotal role. This should not only improve resource allocation but should allow lowering taxes. In the long-run, such public-private infrastructure funds will be more likely to reignite economic growth than newly-created sovereign wealth funds to protect national industries from foreign ownership, as Sarkozy has advocated. The retrenchment of the private sector may be recorded, one day, as the biggest casualty of the economic crisis.

To implement the UK's Financial Services Authority (FSA) as a role model for financial regulation across the G20. No financial regulatory body will come out of the current crisis untarnished. But the FSA is as good as it gets. The FSA's *authority* must be re-capitalized with additional independent powers – similar to that of central bank independence. Financial regulation that is principles-based and encourages self-regulation, overall, has proven to be more effective. In Europe, the

European Union should integrate financial markets regulation across the EURO zone. This is probably the one area where supranational integration could have made a difference to the unfolding of the current crisis. The US has become a caricature of an unsustainably costly and fragmented regulatory system that is compromising the US capital markets' long-term competitiveness. Structural reform of existing regulations rather than more regulation must be the focus.

Political leadership has to be prepared to dare the *Improbable* – as Dubai once did to survive. If governments do not fundamentally reconsider prevalent fiscal and regulatory approaches, citizens are likely to *Exit*. The frustration of those left behind in the West – and the number is likely to increase as a result of the evolving economic crisis – is directed against capitalism's modern bête noire: globalization. The true culprit, however, is a political system that has belittled the individual to a level where self-confidence and faith in the future have been compromised by the politics of fear – fear of terrorism, fear of China, fear of immigration, fear of globalization, fear of failure, and now fear of economic depression.

The Keynesian policy prescription of fiscal expansion and monetary easing blended with regulatory activism – as appears to be now the dominant crisis response across the G-20 – can do no more than alleviate imbalances in the short-term, at best. In the long-run, it is likely to be the cause of future imbalances. The West is challenged to re-define the meaning of economic liberty as we are striving to balance the individual's drive for private wealth creation against the collective's regulatory mandate. Without the historical perspective it is difficult to see how the modern world has effectively turned into a cage, full of limits, suffocating economic liberty. John Maynard Keynes's account of economic reality prior to the outbreak of the Great War in 1914 is worth recalling.

Today, the world's emotional deprecation of the financial services sector, unleashed by a self-inflicted crisis, embeds the danger of a serious mental setback. What is challenged is the individual's 'degradation of the mind before the *Improbable*', the readiness to question, to dare, and to risk unchartered territories rather than to just simply accept given choices and boundaries. And in modern times few places other than Dubai have demonstrated so markedly this readiness to dare the *Improbable*. It is this spirit that is the most promising guarantor to deliver eventually something truly new, saving us from repetition in futility. It is this spirit that should define an agenda for fundamental reform of prevalent governance and fiscal models, beyond crisis management.

"Time, events, or the unaided individual action of the mind will sometimes undermine or destroy an opinion, without any outward sign of change. It has not been openly assailed, no conspiracy has been formed to make war on it, but its followers one by one noiselessly secede; day by day a few of them abandon it, until at last it is only professed by a minority. In this state it will still continue to prevail. As its enemies remain mute or only interchange their thoughts by stealth, they are themselves unaware for a long period that a great revolution has actually been effected; and in this state of uncertainty they take no steps; they observe one another and are silent. The majority have ceased to believe what they believed before, but they still affect to believe, and this empty phantom of public opinion is strong enough to chill innovators and to keep them silent and at a respectful distance", writes Alexis de Tocqueville in 'Democracy in America'.[127]

It all depends on what each one of us will make out of it: *Exit, Voice and Loyalty*.

Hendrik Krawen, *Adam und Eva*, 2005

"But now let us quickly drop down in our plane towards the river. From close up, we can see it is a real river, with rippling waves like a sea. A strong wind is blowing and there are little crests of foam on the waves. Look carefully at the millions of shimmering white bubbles rising and then vanishing with each wave. Over and over again, new bubbles come to the surface and then vanish in time with the waves. For a brief instant they are lifted on the wave's crest and then they sink down and are seen no more. We are like that. Each one of us no more than a tiny glimmering thing, a sparkling droplet on the waves of time which flow past beneath us into an unknown, misty future. We leap up, look around us and, before we know it, we vanish again. We can hardly be seen in the great river of time. New drops keep rising to the surface. And what we call our fate is no more than our struggle in that great multitude of droplets in the rise and fall of one wave. But we must make use of that moment. It is worth the effort."

E.H. Gombrich, *A Little History of the World (1936)*

Endnotes

[1] Indeed, the US is unique in that matter, too. Barack Obama: "For as long as I live, I will never forget that in no other country on earth is my story even possible." as quoted in Roger Cohen, 'American Stories', International Herald Tribune, October 30, 2008

[2] Richard Florida, 'Who's Your City: How the Creative Economy is Making Where to Live the Most Important Decision of Your Life'

[3] Reference is made to US conglomerate Halliburton and its announcement in 2007 to move part of its CEO's office to Dubai.

[4] In this context, the term is borrowed from Richard Florida.

[5] John Lukacs, 'At the End of an Age', p. 78: "Historians are not to be blamed for the intellectual and mental and spiritual crisis at the end of the Modern Age, of which the bureaucratization of intellectual professions, including historianship, is but a consequence. But they ought to be blamed for their ignorance of (or lack of interest in) an amazing condition: the relatively recent development of a spreading appetite for history in the world, something that exists contrary to so many other superficial symptoms." "Historical thinking has entered our very blood." (Johan Huizinga, 1935) in Lukacs, p. 83

[6] Jacques Barzun, 'From Dawn to Decadence', p. 799

[7] According to the Statistics Center of Dubai (Government of Dubai) the population of Dubai amounted to 1,422m by the end of 2006, up from 1,130m in 2005. (Source: 'Dubai in Figures', Statistics Center of Dubai, 2007)

[8] 'Dubai in Figures', Statistics Center of Dubai, 2007

[9] Frauke Heard-Bey, 'From Trucial States to United Arab Emirates', p. 247

[10] Herbert Marcuse, 'One-Dimensional Man'

[11] William Safire, 'How can you be naked wearing shorts?', International Herald Tribune, October 6, 2008: "Sometime ahead, when the toxicity dissipates and the bailout pays off, we can expect a breezy new metaphor for the economic outlook: a brisk new tailwind (coined in 1897), causing much flapping of the naked shorts."

[12] Mancur Olson, 'Power and Prosperity', p. 178: "…market-contrary policies always generate large shadow economies and lots of corruption in government."

[13] Simeon Kerr and Andrew England, 'Moody's warns on Dubai vulnerability', Financial Times, October 12, 2008

[14] Simeon Kerr and Roula Khalaf, 'Analysis: A high debt burden risks leaving Dubai up the creek', Financial Times, April 3, 2008

[15] Simeon Kerr, 'Detained banker 'tortured' in Dubai', Financial Times, June 9, 2008

[16] Simeon Kerr, 'UK raises UAE terrorism risk level to 'high'', Financial Times, June 17, 2008

[17] John Lukacs, 'At the End of an Age', pp. 142-143: "This is what Jakob Burckhardt meant, more than 130 years ago, when he said that "happiness is to be found in our misfortunes, it can only be a spiritual one: to be turned facing the past so as to save the culture of former times, and facing the future so as to give an example of the spiritual in an age which might otherwise succumb entirely to the material." "…from a spiritual thirst or hunger that arises at the end of an age, and that materialism cannot satisfy."

[18] Jacques Barzun, 'From Dawn to Decadence', p. 799

[19] Zygmunt Bauman, 'Liquid Modernity', p. 10

[20] John Lukacs, 'At the End of an Age', p. 39

[21] Samuel Huntington, 'The Clash of Civilizations?' reprinted in 'The Debate', p. 17, The Council on Foreign Relations, 1996: "The very notion that there could be a 'universal civilization' is a Western idea, directly at odds with the particularism of most Asian societies and their emphasis on what distinguishes one people from another."

[22] Ibid, p. 1

[23] David Fromkin, 'Europe's Last Summer', p. 13

[24] Thérèse Delpech, 'Savage Century: Back to Barbarism', p. 6

[25] J. Ortega y Gasset, 'Le Rebelión de las Masas', Madrid, 1930 (English translation: The Revolt of the Masses). In his famous 'diagnosis of our time', the Spanish philosopher proclaimed that the most important fact of the contemporary epoch was the rise of the masses. "It may be said that the age of democracy has, in reality, devolved into the age of bureaucracy." (Lukacs, p. 19)

[26] "The twentieth century was a transitional century (as was a century at the end of the Middle Ages, from about 1450 to 1550) – in every sense, the twentieth was also a short century, lasting from 1914 to 1989, seventy-five years. After that, the collapse of Communism (and of the Russian Empire) did not lead to a conservative reaction: the symptoms of dissolution continued – indeed, many of them gathered speed during the last decade of the chronological twentieth century (no fin-de-siècle then). No, history is not a mechanical clock: the pendulum never swings back. But human events and minds change, though slowly; something different, something new is beginning." (Lukacs, p. 29)

[27] The Economist, 'Kohl's Kingdom', p. 11, March 24, 1990

[28] Financial Times, 'Perestroika minus glasnost', March 16, 1992

[29] Quentin Peel, 'Visionary despised in his own land', Financial Times, August 20, 1991

[30] Quoted in Serge Schmemann, 'A Land of Extremes, Awesome Even in Death', International Herald Tribune, December 26, 1991

[31] Jeffrey Sachs and Charles Wyplosz, 'How the West Should Help Russian Reform', Financial Times, January 11, 1994; see also Bijan Khezri, 'Finance not the key to Russian reform', Financial Times, January 13, 1994

[32] 'US Launches $4bn Fund to Aid Russian Privatization', Financial Times, April 15, 1993

[33] Chrysta Freeland, 'Sale of the Century: The Inside Story of the Second Russian Revolution'

[34] In July 1990, at the Russian resort spa of Zheleznovodsk Kohl and Gorbatchev had swept aside the last significant obstacles to uniting Germany by the end of that year.

[35] Bruce W. Nelan, 'Kohl Wins His Way', p. 26, Time Magazine, New York, July 30, 1990

[36] Ibid

[37] Bijan Khezri, 'The End of an Age in Europe', Wall Street Journal, June 1, 2005

[38] The Economist, 'Ireland's voters speak', June 21, 2008

[39] Charlemagne, 'Democracy in Europe', The Economist, June 21, 2008

[40] Samuel Brittan, 'Why the Irish were right to say No', Financial Times, June 20, 2008

[41] Ibid

[42] Roger Cohen, 'Sarkozy surfs the USA', International Herald Tribune, August 6, 2007

[43] Stefan Theil, 'Europe's Philosophy of Failure', Foreign Policy, January/February, 2008

[44] Ibid

[45] Gideon Rachman, 'Super-Sarko's plans for the world', Financial Times, October 20, 2008: 'Mr Sarkozy wants a crackdown on international tax havens. The idea of "unfair tax competition between nations has long been a bugbear of the French." In fact, the financial crisis will further question the relevance of the EU since a vacuum of supranational financial market supervision has been exposed, forcing national governments to lead the way on their own– rather than through EU institutions.

[46] His image rather than substance is President Sarkozy's primary concern. In October 2008 a French court rejected Sarkozy's argument that a voodoo doll bearing his name violated his right to his own image. 'Nicolas Sarkozy: The Voodoo Manuel' – a kit including a hand-book, 12 pins and a blue-colored voodoo doll – is for sale at EUR 12.95.

[47] 'Parce qu'il a abandonné sa fonction d'autorité au profit du pouvoir qu'elle lui confère, et que, de ce fait, il s'est approché de nous, de gré ou de force, sans que plus rien nous sépare. Jusqu'à devenir un personnage familier, presque domestique, qui entre dans notre intimité.' in Serge Hefez, 'La Sarkose obsessionnelle', p. 54

[48] Serge Hefez quoted in Steven Erlanger, 'New ailment afflicts the French – obsessive Sarkosis', International Herald Tribune, May 24-25, 2008

[49] 'Sustaining New York's and the US' Global Financial Services Leadership', The City of New York, Office of the Mayor, 2007

[50] Francis Fukuyama, 'The End of History and the Last Man'

51 Samuel Huntington, 'The Clash of Civilizations', Foreign Affairs, Summer 1993

52 William J. Dobson, 'The Day Nothing Much Changed', Foreign Policy, September/October, 2006

53 Arnon Gutfeld, 'American Exceptionalism', p. 91

54 Ibid

55 As quoted in Megan Riley McGilchrist, 'With Susan Sontag, America lost a conscience', International Herald Tribune, January 18, 2005

56 A survey of over 28,000 respondents across 27 countries was conducted for the BBC World Service by the international polling firm GlobeScan with the Program on International Policy Attitudes (PIPA) at the University of Maryland. GlobeScan coordinated the fieldwork between November 2006 and January 2007. The poll was published on February 16, 2007

57 Ian Buruma and Avishai Margalit, 'Occidentalism', p. 147

58 Zachary Karabell, 'City of Dreams', Wall Street Journal, March 17, 2007

59 David Fromkin, 'The Way of the World', p. 218

60 Ibid, p. 186

61 Fouad Ajami, 'The Summoning', Foreign Affairs, September/October, 1993: "Contrast the way Huntington sees things with Braudel's depiction of the traffic between Christendom and Islam across the Mediterranean in the sixteenth century – and this was in a religious age, after the fall of Constantinople to the Turks and of Granada to the Spanish: "Men passed to and fro, indifferent to frontiers, states and creeds. They were more aware of the necessities for shipping and trade, the hazards of war and piracy, the opportunities for complicity or betrayal provided by circumstances." [Ferdinand Braudel, 'The Mediterranean and the Mediterranean World in the Age of Philip II', p. 759, New York, 1957]

62 As quoted in David Brooks, 'Too early to count Blair out', International Herald Tribune, May 12, 2007

63 Ibid

64 Samuel Huntington, 'If not civilizations, what? – Paradigms of the Post-Cold War World' in 'The Clash of Civilizations? – The Debate', p. 66, The Council on Foreign Relations, 1996

65 Richard Florida has produced a number of graphical illustrations of the world's spikiness in terms of population, economic activity, and innovation. See Richard Florida, 'Who's your City?'

66 Thomas L. Friedman, 'Is the World Flat?', Letters, Foreign Policy, May/June 2007

67 Development costs are estimated at US$25-27bn.

68 'Sustaining New York's and the US' Global Financial Services Leadership', The City of New York, Office of the Mayor, 2007

69 According to the report the "flawed implementation of the 2002 Sarbanes-Oxley Act (SOX), which produced far heavier costs than expected, has only aggravated the situation…"

70 Oswald Spengler, 'The Decline of the West', p. 3

71 Mark Mazower, 'Do not Mourn the End of the West', Financial Times, May 28, 2003

72 Arnon Gutfeld, 'American Exceptionalism', Preface

73 Ibid

74 George Rogers Taylor, 'The Turner Thesis', p. 3, Lexington (MA), 1972

75 Frederick Jackson Turner, 'The Significance of the Frontier in American History', in John Mack Faragher (ed.), 'Rereading Frederick Jackson Turner', pp.11-30, New Haven, 1994

76 Arnon Gutfeld, 'American Exceptionalism', p.35

77 For a review see Arnon Gutfeld, 'American Exceptionalism', p.76

78 Ibid

79 Arnon Gutfeld, 'American Exceptionalism', Preface

80 Sacvan Bercovitch, 'The Rites of Assent: Transformations in the Symbolic Construction of America, p. 29, New York, 1993

[81] Ibid, p. 41

[82] Ibid, p. 33

[83] Ibid, p. 35

[84] Around the 7th century AD Arabic-speaking Umayyads arrived to spread Islam among the locals. "Islam was the indestructible, lasting fabric into whose even structure the pattern of local historical events was printed."(Frauke Heard-Bey, 'From Trucial States to United Arab Emirates', p. 135)

[85] The Venetian jeweler Gasparo Balbi, attracted by the region's sunny climate and shallow waters for pearling, provided the first written reference to the city as 'Dibei' when he toured the region in 1580. For a summary of the history of Dubai, see The Economist City Guide (which is frequently updated online). For a more in-depth and comprehensive historical insight see Frauke Heard-Bey's classic historiogram 'From Trucial States to United Arab Emirates'. For an insightful, multifaceted and critical perspective of modern Dubai see the Spring/Summer 2005 edition of the cultural magazine BIDOUN. The issue is dedicated to Dubai.

[86] The Economist City Guide, 'Dubai', www.economist.com, October 2008

[87] Ibid

[88] John Lorimer, 'History of the Persian Gulf', as quoted in Graeme Wilson, 'Rashid's Legacy: The Genesis of the Maktoum Family and the History of Dubai', p. 38

[89] Graeme Wilson, 'Rashid's Legacy: The Genesis of the Maktoum Family and the History of Dubai', p. 49

[90] Ibid, p.56

[91] Ibid, p.52

[92] Frauke Heard-Bey, 'From Trucial States to United Arab Emirates', p. 271

[93] Ibid

[94] Uniting first six and then seven of the nine Trucial states. Oman and Bahrain chose independence. The seventh and most northern of all Trucial states, Ra's al Khaimah, did not join until some time after the Federation had been proclaimed. According to Frauke Heard-Bey "Ra's al Khaimah had resented that throughout the negotiations between the nine States it did not rank equal with the big four." (p. 369)

[95] As quoted in Graeme Wilson, 'Rashid's Legacy: The Genesis of the Maktoum Family and the History of Dubai', p. 37

[96] Ibid, pp. 37-38

[97] Christopher Davidson, 'Dubai: The Vulnerabilities of Success', p. 178

[98] As quoted in Gulf News, 'I will give you pride and glory: Mohammad', February 4, 2007

[99] Zygmunt Bauman, 'Liquid Modernity', p. 9

[100] Dubai Chamber of Commerce & Industry, '1000 Numbers & Reasons Why Dubai', p. 33, Beirut, 2006

[101] Gulf News, 'Burj Dubai sets global records', July 22, 2007

[102] For a comprehensive overview of construction projects visit: www.sheikhmohammed.ae

[103] Frauke Heard-Bey, 'From Trucial States to United Arab Emirates', p. 247

[104] Christopher Davidson, 'Dubai: The Vulnerabilities of Success', p. 182

[105] Oil fields were not discovered and developed until the 1960s, and oil was first exported in 1969, seven years later than Abu Dhabi.

[106] Dubai Chamber of Commerce & Industry, '1000 Numbers & Reasons Why Dubai', p. 32, Beirut 2006

[107] Gulf Business, 'Dubai's Dream Run', July 2007

[108] Carter Dougherty, 'Europe acts to protect state-run interests', International Herald Tribune, July 14, 2007

[109] Gulf Business, 'Dubai's Dream Run', July 2007

[110] When in March 2007 the Government announced that Umm Suqeim beach, one of the last remaining public beaches in Dubai, would close to make way for another beachfront property development, an unprecedented wave of protest and complaints was set in motion. One month later, Sheikh Mohamed bin Rashid Al

Maktoum, Dubai's ruler, ordered an end to the construction project. A rare U-turn, but testimony that public places are valued and the opinion of expatriates matters. See Simeon Kerr, 'Dubai's Ruler turns tide on beach development', The Financial Times, April 24, 2007

[111] 'Dubai in Figures', Statistics Center of Dubai, 2007

[112] "The most common complaint from construction workers in the UAE, which also appears to form the basis of the vast majority of labor disputes reviewed by the Ministry of Labor and the Dubai labor agencies, is the withholding of wages by employers. All 60 of the workers interviewed by Human Rights Watch said that their employers routinely withheld their wages, and many of the workers we spoke to were owed back wages at the time of the interview. The impact on workers whose wages are withheld for even one month is very serious: they immediately fall into arrears on the debt they owe recruiting agencies in their home countries; they incur additional interest; and they are unable to send money home to their families, who depend on the income earned in the UAE. In some cases, the non-payment of wages means that workers do not have money to buy food or basic goods and end up borrowing money just to survive. Withholding one-and-a-half or two months' wages as 'security' to prevent workers from 'running away' to a better job appears to be accepted as a 'custom' among construction companies in the UAE.", 'UAE: Workers abused in construction boom', Human Rights Watch (www.hrw.org), November 12, 2006

[113] Dan McDougall, 'Tourists become targets as Dubai's workers take revolt to the beaches', The Observer, August 9, 2006

[114] 'Workers die in Dubai tower fire', BBC News 24, January 18, 2007

[115] Lucy Williamson, 'Migrants' woes in Dubai worker camps', BBC News 24, February 10, 2005

[116] "In the past few years, the media has reported several cases of suicide of construction workers distressed about their working conditions. Accurate and reliable data on the number of suicides are, of course, hard to come by. According to Syed Mubarak, labor attaché at the Indian consulate in Dubai, 84 Indian nationals committed suicide in 2005 alone, although it is not clear how many of these cases involved construction workers." in 'UAE: Workers abused in construction boom', Human Rights Watch (www.hrw.org), November 12, 2006

[117] Avdesh, Dubai worker, as quoted in Lucy Williamson, 'Migrants' woes in Dubai worker camps', BBC News 24, February 10, 2005

[118] The lawsuit was filed in Miami because the members of the royal family maintain hundreds of horses at farms in Ocala in Florida.

[119] The UAE has more than two million camels, almost twice the population of Dubai, the UAE's most populous city. Camel races are among the most popular sports events in the country and take place between October and April. A camel from a 'prize-winning bloodline' can sell for as much as US$1 million. It is a big business.

[120] Curt Anderson, 'Dubai leaders seek jockey suit dismissal', Associated Press, July 16, 2007

[121] The Emirates set up a program with UNICEF to reunite the children with their families and provide a range of social and educational services. In addition, the Ruler of Dubai launched a number of initiatives to not only enforce labor laws but to improve workers' living conditions.

[122] Zygmunt Bauman, 'Liquid Times', p. 98

[123] Mancur Olson, 'Power and Prosperity', p.100: "There also has been spectacular growth under a few autocrats (such as Taiwan, South Korea, Singapore, China and Chile) in relatively recent times. The economically most successful autocrats not only tend to have long planning horizons but also resist or repress special-interest groups: they tend to have 'hard' states that do not usually adapt their policies to organized interests in particular occupations or industries."

[124] Ackley, Brian, 'Permanent Vacation: Dubai Circa 2005', p.39, in Basar, Shumon and Carver, Antonia and Markus Miessen, eds. 'With/Without: Spatial Products, Practices & Politics in the Middle East', Bidoun Book, Dubai, 2007

[125] Ian Buruma and Avishai Margalit, 'Occidentalism', p. 19

[126] Everett Ehrlich and Felix G. Rohatyn, 'A New Bank to Save Our Infrastructure', The New York Review of Books, Volume 55, Number 15, October 9, 2008

[127] Alexis de Tocqueville, 'Democracy in America', pp. 321-22, Cambridge (MA), 1863 (www.books.google.com)

Selected Bibliography

Barzun, Jacques, 'From Dawn to Decadence', New York, 2000

Barzun, Jacques, 'The Culture We Deserve', Connecticut, 1989

Bauman, Zygmunt, 'Liquid Modernity', Massachusetts, 2006

Bauman, Zygmunt, 'Liquid Times', Massachusetts, 2007

Bercovitch, Sacvan, 'The Rites of Assent: Transformations in the Symbolic Construction of America', New York, 1993

Buruma, Ian and Avishai Margalit, 'Occidentalism: The West in the Eyes of Its Enemies', New York, 2004

Cioran, Emile M., 'A Short History of Decay', New York, 1975 (English translation by Richard Howard of "Précis de decomposition" published in 1949 by Editions Gallimard)

Davidson, Christopher, 'Dubai: The Vulnerabilities of Success', New York, 2008

Delpech, Thérèse, 'Savage Century: Back to Barbarism', Washington (DC), 2007 (Originally published under the title 'L'Ensauvagement: Le retour de la barbarie au XXIe siècle' in Paris in 2005)

Florida, Richard, 'Who's Your City: How the Creative Economy is Making Where to Live the Most Important Decision of Your Life', Philadelphia, 2008

Freeland, Chrysta, 'Sale of the Century: The Inside Story of the Second Russian Revolution', London, 2002

Fromkin, David, 'The Way of the World', New York, 1998

Fromkin, David, 'Europe's Last Summer', New York, 2005

Fukuyama, Francis, 'The End of History and the Last Man', New York, 1992

Gombrich, E.H., 'A Little History of the World', Cambridge (UK), 2005 (Originally published under the title 'Weltgeschichte von der Urzeit bis zur Gegenwart' in Vienna in 1936)

Gutfeld, Arnon, 'American Exceptionalism', Brighton (UK), 2002

Heard-Bey, Frauke, 'From Trucial States to United Arab Emirates', Ajman (United Arab Emirates), 2004 (first published in 1982)

Hefez, Serge, 'La Sarkose obsessionnelle', Paris, 2008

Hirschman, Albert O., 'Exit, Voice and Loyalty: Responses to Decline in Firms, Organizations, and States', Cambridge (MA), 1970

Huntington, Samuel, 'The Clash of Civilizations', Foreign Affairs, Summer 1993

Lukacs, John, 'At the End of an Age', New Haven, 2002

Macfarlane, Alan, 'The Riddle of the Modern World: Of Liberty, Wealth and Equality', New York, 2000

Macfarlane, Alan, 'The Making of the Modern World: Visions from the West and East', New York, 2002

Marcuse, Herbert, 'One-Dimensional Man', Boston, 1964

Moore, Robin, 'Dubai', Garden City, 1976

Olson, Mancur, 'Power and Prosperity', New York, 2000

Riesman, David (with Nathan Glazer and Reuel Denney), 'The Lonely Crowd', New Haven, 2001 (first published in 1953)

Spengler, Oswald, 'The Decline of the West', English Abridged Edition prepared by Arthur Helps, from the translation by Charles Francis Atkinson, New York, 1991 (Originally published as 'Der Untergang des Abendlandes, Gestalt und Wirklichkeit' in 1918)

Wilson, Graeme, 'Rashid's Legacy: The Genesis of the Maktoum Family and the History of Dubai', Dubai, 2006